Doctor in the Navy

Doctor in the Navy

Bill Yule

To Jasmine, a delightful granddaughter

Published by
Whittles Publishing,
Dunbeath,
Caithness KW6 6EG,
Scotland, UK

www.whittlespublishing.com

© 2010 Bill Yule

ISBN 978-184995-001-5

Printed by 4edge Limited, UK

Contents

Preface

National service, Britain's term for conscription, existed between 1945 and 1963. During that time, two and a half million men were required to serve with the armed forces for a period of two years. For some, it was a miserable penance. For the majority, it was just something that had to be done because of one's date of birth. For a lucky few, of whom I was one, it was a time of travel and adventure.

One had the option of joining up at the age of seventeen or, if one elected to do so, enlistment could be postponed until completion of education or a course of training. I had decided on a medical degree and the undergraduate course at that time lasted for six years. With a further year of houseman posts required before full registration, it was thus seven years before I was let loose on the public. In this case, 'the public' was necessarily the armed forces.

The story of my national service is told from notes made, and letters written, at the time. This may explain some of the overly-exuberant comments and, of course, my recent freedom from long medical training had to be celebrated.

As the time for national service drew near, I was unsure of which of the many paths within medicine I would take. As will be seen, the forthcoming months were to prove useful in reaching a decision.

When the time eventually arrived for enlistment, the Navy, being a smaller Service, required only a few doctors. Learning this was a blow, as I was not particularly keen to go into the Army or the RAF. It was decided, by the powers-that-be, that entry into the Navy was to be by selection after interview. Accordingly those of us who had opted for the Navy, trooped down to London to be interviewed by a Senior Naval Person.

When my turn came I was asked, 'If we take you, what sort of posting would you like?' My answer 'Small ships abroad, please' appeared to go down well, and I was accepted. I felt sorry for those who were not so lucky and had to go to the other Services.

Bill Yule

1

Edinburgh Royal Infirmary

'**P**ut him up in modified Russell Traction,' said the senior surgical registrar, 'and I will pin him in the morning.' Modified Russell Traction? My fellow house surgeon and I had no idea what he meant. It was, however, our first 'admitting night' and we were not keen to admit to our ignorance. After all, we had six years of medical school and six months of house physician experience behind us. We noticed Sister Blythe glancing at us quizzically from behind the surgeon's back. 'I'll show you,' she whispered, and our pride was saved.

The prospect of working in an acute surgical unit at Edinburgh Royal Infirmary was initially a daunting experience. I was very conscious of the reputation of this hospital and the changes that would have to be made from the carefree student days of my last time there, to the very busy days of a working doctor charged with a fair amount of responsibility. I had spent my six months as a house physician in a smaller hospital and although the responsibility was just as great, there was much less feeling of a need to excel. Only a renowned teaching hospital put this kind of pressure on those working in it. Although, one might not have thought that this was the case from the brief informality of my interview for the job.

The 'Chief' (the senior surgeon of the unit) was working in what was called the Diagnostic Theatre when I arrived. Clad in a white operating kit, he looked at me over gold-rimmed glasses, balanced on the end of his nose, and asked me only two questions: 'Are you qualified?' and 'Who are you working for just now?' He seemed satisfied with my answers on both counts and remarked that my present boss, a consultant physician, was known to him and was 'a good man'. 'Right,' he concluded, 'you start at the beginning of next month.' As this was only two weeks away, any hopes I might have had of a holiday were dashed. He then returned to his cystoscopy and I left the theatre, both pleased and a little apprehensive.

So now we were at the sharp end: responsible for all the admissions to, and problems of, the unit. I was in one of the three surgical units situated on the most formally decorated of the Infirmary's corridors. Unlike the stone floors throughout the rest of the hospital, here there was immaculate black and white linoleum. While there were other surgical units, those on the 'Black and White Corridor' shared the prestige of being at the heart of operations. Here hung elaborate boards listing the donors who bequeathed funds to Edinburgh's hospital, long before the NHS was thought up. Located here were the main administration and nursing offices, and here too was where important visitors were entertained. Some of this prestige was bound to rub off on even the newest recruit.

I quickly learned just how important it was to be on good terms with the ward sister. In addition to explaining, in the case above, exactly what 'Modified Russell Traction' was (it is a means of temporarily immobilising a fractured neck of femur), she also helped us to set it up, so that the old man being operated on was comfortable before the time-consuming operation he was to undergo the following day. She remained helpful on many other occasions, but the majority of the sisters were not so houseman-friendly. Often we were regarded as the lowest of the low, and a bit of a nuisance besides. One such lady greeted me with 'When you take blood don't make a mess of the sheets. If you want to go round with me (I never did) be here by eight o'clock sharp.'

At first, being considered less than competent felt bad. Inevitably, my skills grew, and by the end of six months I had mastered all the work of a surgical house officer. Thanks to the younger surgeons in the unit, and to patient anaesthetists, I had even removed a few appendices. The latter gave me immense pleasure, as did being left alone to close wounds following

House Officers, Edinburgh Royal Infirmary, summer 1957. The author is forth from the right in the back row

other doctors' operations and repairing minor lacerations in the glamorous surroundings of an Edinburgh Royal operating theatre.

There was, of course, a down side, or rather two down sides, to the work: first the anaesthetist and then the senior surgeon. It was not the hospital's policy to employ theatre porters, as their work was done by the house surgeons. This meant that if one was delayed in finishing a case, having been left to close a wound, there would be a resultant delay in producing the next patient. Under such conditions, I might be required to help lift the first man from the operating table on to a trolley, push the trolley back to the ward, see him safely handed over to the ward nurses, then load the next patient/victim on to the same trolley, and push it back to theatre. By this time, the anaesthetist was champing at the bit waiting for his patient as he, in his turn, would have to face the wrath of the surgeon. The latter, known for his short temper, was ferocious on occasion. One of my predecessors had warned me before I started. 'Wait till he does his first prostatectomy!' he said, 'remember it's your job to tie the bag on the Foley while he does other things, and he has no patience. You'll be so scared that you're bound to get it wrong first time, and then Heaven help you!' This dire warning was to be proven true.

The one person who could handle this able but irascible man was his theatre sister, who had worked with him for many years. One story about the two goes as follows. The surgeon, who was impatient, could not get a pair of artery forceps to grip. He tossed them up into the open students' gallery and held out his hand for another pair, breathing heavily. The Sister passed him another pair but, again, he could not get it to grip and threw it after the first. The Sister knew the fault was his and not that of the instruments. She picked up a further pair of forceps and then threw it after his. She then handed him yet another pair and said 'Your turn, sir!' He stood there, stunned for a moment, and then laughed.

The same man was known throughout the hospital for the seemingly innocuous habit of having a boiled egg for his lunch on operating days. This was, however, a habit which led to his house officers being subject to much leg-pulling from colleagues who worked in units overlooking the car park. The story became known as 'The Chief's Egg'. It was his practice to bring an egg to the hospital on his operating days. This was placed carefully under the

4

central rear armrest of his car, where it was then forgotten about, or more likely, ignored. All senior surgeons were met by those of their staff who were free and then walked along the corridor to their wards. Conversation was inevitably a little stilted, but easier in this case because the great man had just been appointed captain of one of East Lothian's golf clubs. He was very proud of this and it was usually possible to work off this appropriate cue. Having reached the ward, he suddenly remembered the egg, and a houseman was given the car keys and sent to fetch it. The unfortunate young man then had to run the gauntlet of ribald remarks from those who knew all about this recurring drama. The egg was then delivered to the ward kitchen, to be prepared with one slice of buttered bread and a glass of milk for the great man's lunch.

Not all the surgeons were bad tempered, however, and the 'sub-chief', the unit's number two, was a pawky Aberdonian. On one occasion, towards the end of my six months, I was assisting him with an appendicectomy. I knew the procedure, having done one or two myself, but when he said 'Hold the appendix up!', I could not see that anything more was needed. I was, I thought, holding the appendix up, ready for the next step. I went over the procedure to myself, decided he had adequate access, and did nothing. Again he said, 'Hold the appendix up!' and I became even more baffled. Deciding that all was well and waiting for him to carry on, I could see no reason to alter what I was doing, and again did nothing, This time he took one step back from the table, folded his gloved hands over his green gowned chest, looked at me over his spectacles, and said quite calmly 'I see you're a man of conviction, Yule!' I never did find out what he wanted, but I was glad that it was he, and not the older man, who was operating that day.

The six months finally came to an end. I had gained much useful experience and had made no serious mistakes. I was soon to exchange the living conditions of a house doctor for those of the Armed Services and, in this respect, Edinburgh Royal Infirmary had an excellent record. Bedrooms were comfortable, quiet and well heated. The dining room, in the charge of a butler, served good food and there was always a supply of biscuits and cheese for those who missed meals. There was also a well organised social life, exclusive to the thirty people who lived in the residency. A formal dinner was held twice every six months, at which there were always two guest speakers. During my time, these were Compton McKenzie and Lord Cameron, a Scottish judge. McKenzie was at that time advertising a blend of Scotch whisky, and an appropriate bottle was thoughtfully placed before him at table. It was the tradition for the night nurse in charge of one's ward to make a tie to go with one's dinner jacket. For the first dinner, my night nurse made me a large, decorated plaster-of-Paris construction which I remember as being heavy. For the second dinner, she made a tie with a little inflatable man in the middle. He was connected by a thin rubber tube, which disappeared behind my collar and finished with a bulb in my trouser pocket. This meant that on squeezing the bulb, the little man waved his arms and legs and squirted water on anyone who came too close. Every member of the mess had to be mentioned in a poem delivered by the Mess Bard at each dinner, and the Keeper of the Virgins was summoned to give an account of the numbers in his care. It was also the tradition to carve one's name on the main mess table. This was replaced every six months and the carved table-tops hung on a wall alongside the twice-yearly mess photograph.

Now my time had arrived to spend two compulsory years on national service. This was a mixed blessing, as, unlike some of my contemporaries, I had not yet decided on which career I wished to pursue within medicine. There was no need for me to decide immediately, and even a permanent career with the forces was a possibility. As time went by, however, the need to make a decision became more pressing.

It was with regret that I left Edinburgh, but before doing so, a local GP, visiting one of his patients in the ward and knowing that the change-over was about to happen, asked me to do a fortnight's locum for him. I thought I had just enough time to do this before going off to the forces, although again it meant giving up a holiday. Two cases in the fortnight showed me the difference between hospital and general practice.

The first of these involved the expected death of an old lady. She had been ill for some time with terminal cancer, but what was unexpected was her husband's reaction to her death. She died about eight o'clock one evening at her home, a high tenement flat on Leith Walk. The flat contained just the two of them, alone in the world. 'I'll phone the undertaker for you,' I said, 'do you know of anyone?' 'No, it's all right,' he replied, 'I'll just keep her here with me.' I explained to him the problems this would cause, but he would not change his mind. I therefore had to leave, but in doing so made him promise to let me in when I came back the next morning. Fortunately, by that time he had realised that he had no option but to agree and give up his wife for burial.

The second case began with a phone call from a man who sounded both rough and drunk. He requested an urgent visit to an address in a notorious area of the city, giving no further details. On arrival at the allotted address, I found an Alsatian dog barring the way to a door at the end of a dark close. This was the oldest of Old Edinburgh. I went around the dog, found the door unlocked and entered to find a young woman alone. She was surprised to see me and at first denied that my services were required. It was too dark to see her properly. Then, as my eyes adjusted to the gloom, I saw that she was distressed. She was leaning with her back to a dirty sink and her hands behind her. The sink was heavily blood-stained and it turned out that she had cut her wrists after a row with the man who had phoned. A quick application of pressure bandages to the wounds and then removal to the Infirmary for stitching was all that was needed. It was interesting to see A & E from the other side.

2

Portsmouth and Chatham

National Service was imminent, but I was left with time, after all, for a short holiday. An instruction to get a navy blue uniform made at a naval tailor was followed by an order to report to the Royal Naval Barracks at Portsmouth.

And so, after a tedious train journey from Scotland, relieved only by Richard Gordon's *Doctor In Love* (which I finished), I arrived at HMS *Victory*, the Navy's name for the 'stone frigate' which up until then was known to me simply as the RNB Portsmouth. Most of the other newly qualified doctors had arrived, a total of twenty, with eight being from my year at Edinburgh.

Our new group of surgeon lieutenants was to be the cause of some hilarity, especially when we took to Portsmouth's parade ground, one of the most famous places in the Navy. Bugles sounded frequently and the square was full, squads being drilled throughout the day. The terrifying roars of the petty officers made it seem a daunting place. What about saluting, we wondered, which people seemed to do all the time. 'Just salute everyone senior to you,' said one of the retired men who acted as mess stewards. The same man had just pulled me up for whistling: 'In the Navy, Sir, we do not whistle.' Apparently this was more than just bad manners, as apparently it could cause confusion with a bosun's pipe. The advice he gave concerning saluting was useful, but easier said than done. What about women, we wondered. The parade ground was full of them, some in raincoats which concealed badges of rank, even had we known what these were. Their hats, all smart, were very confusing. The answer, it seemed, was to salute everyone, on some occasions to their surprise. After all, what did it matter? We had to be there anyway and nobody expected us to know anything, so we resolved to enjoy ourselves.

There then followed a trek around the various departments. The amount of kit issued was immense. How it was all to be carried was certainly a problem, but this became a minor worry with the start of the Officers' Divisional Course. This was part of the usual initiation for national service recruits. We were just the right number to form one group, attending an intensive course in things both practical and obscurely theoretical. We were in the charge of a booted and gaitered chief petty officer (CPO) sporting an impressive array of medal ribbons. He addressed us as 'Sir' but didn't mean it, especially when he saw us on the drill square. 'Everyone who comes into the Navy must learn to march and handle a boat,' he said. Looking around me I understood why he looked a little sceptical. We were indeed a mixed bunch, with some of us looking decidedly unmilitary.

The lectures were interesting and the subject of an examination. Rumour had it that the people with the best marks were to receive the best postings. This proved false, as did all the other rumours circulated, such as one which claimed that as we were only temporarily in the Navy, we would be handed the less attractive jobs. Examples given were MO to the Reserve Fleet, holiday relief, and so on – the duller the better.

We learned many things in a short time, some useful and some not. For instance, did we really need to know that a stoker, 5th class, must wear buttons of black horn and not brass? Did we really need to know how to greet the officer of the watch when going aboard a Turkish warship? On the other hand, the course was certainly thorough and I was to find out later just how useful it had been.

Our day started at seven in the morning and we were on the parade ground for 'Divisions' by eight. This included the inspection of uniforms and the hoisting of the Union Jack, to remind us that we were now in the British armed forces. Then, there was an hour of drill which we found hilarious, but this was very much not the case for our CPO. It was he, of course, who, in limited time, had to convert our motley group of twenty medics into a group who were, at the least very least, able to stop and start at approximately the same time. To be fair to him, and to everyone's satisfaction, he actually achieved this aim.

When it came to marching, the learning process was good fun, an entertaining way to spend the cold winter mornings. The most ineducable among us had the unfortunate habit of putting the same side's arm and leg forward and backward at the same time. This is actually quite difficult to do when one thinks about it and is not, of course, what one does during normal walking. It follows that it is even less desirable to do when marching and it was this, above all else, which drove our CPO to despair. He would curse under his breath and then attempt to explain the problem to the wrongdoer, all the while calling him 'Sir', which must have hurt the recruit's ego. Another man's enthusiasm got the better of him. This man marched with his shoulders drawn right up and, as he wore braces instead of a trouser belt, the result was that his trousers were also drawn up to a remarkable height, revealing lengths of black sock covering thin ankles. This earned him a spluttering telling off from the CPO.

There was much mirth when we took turns at drilling each other. Our two problems of saluting and marching came together on one wet day when we emerged from a covered drill shed. A small, newly entered rating came unexpectedly around the corner. The man in charge of us reacted with commendable alacrity. 'Eyes right!' he bellowed, and while we did so, he saluted the surprised rating. This earned the comment, 'That was a very smart salute, Sir, but next time remember that he salutes you, not the other way round.'

Discipline plays an important role in Service life and as divisional officers – that is officers in charge of the lower ranks, which was the sickbay staff in our case – it was necessary to know how the adversarial style of naval justice operated. Ten small episodes of 'Captain's Defaulters' were enacted, with the members of the course acting the parts. I was a leading stoker, accused of swearing at an officer, and one of the others was a 'Jack Dusty', or an able cook, who was supposed to have witnessed the offence. Adoption of regional accents, in this case Cornish, added to the fun.

One afternoon we were taken to a small brick hut in the grounds, which was labelled 'Gas Chamber'. We were given respirators and then told to take them off so that we might know what tear gas was like. It is potent.

Life in the officers' mess at RNB Portsmouth was very comfortable, with excellent food served amongst splendid surroundings. Mess bills were high. The bedrooms, or 'cabins' as they were inevitably known, were heated by open coal fires, which must have entailed much work for some poor servant – an almost Dickensian task. The ship analogy was almost carried too far. For example, one 'went ashore' instead of 'into the town'. It was interesting to be shown over the old *Victory*, which was still used by the commander-in-chief for formal dinners. Other ships in port included *Vanguard,* five aircraft carriers, the Royal Yacht and several cruisers and frigates. The destroyer *Vigo* was also in port and arrangements were made for us to be shown around her. We took a long time over this, as it was the first time we had been on a warship.

This visit to *Vigo* came at the end of our stay in Portsmouth and was helpful in allowing us feel a little less out of place in this new and very different environment. The Navy had done well in demonstrating its operation to a bunch of new recruits. It was certainly a tribute to those who had organised the course.

It was now time to move on. Half of us were assigned to HMS *Drake* at Plymouth and half were sent to HMS *Pembroke,* another stone frigate, this time at Chatham. I was sent to Chatham for what was meant to be an introduction to naval medicine and where the pace of events was much slower. Some of the non-medical training was, however, great fun.

We arrived on a grim, grey Sunday in the grim, grey town of Chatham, Kent. I did not remember ever being in a grimmer place. If Kent was the garden of England, I thought, then this must be the compost heap. The Naval Hospital, which has a long and honourable history, was situated pleasantly. It sits on a hill overlooking the town, with lawns, grass tennis courts and a cricket pitch. It was a relief to escape from the grim urban landscape into the grounds of this relaxing place. Chatham is continuous with Gillingham and is seventy miles from London. Strood, Rochester, Chatham and Gillingham are known as the Medway towns.

Portsmouth – the author is third from the right in the back row

The exam results arrived from Portsmouth and I got seventy-three per cent, with nobody achieving less than fifty-five per cent. The significance of these figures, it had been decided, was exactly nil, but it had certainly helped in concentrating our knowledge, which was probably its objective.

Our stay at Chatham was supposed to be an introduction to naval medicine, but this turned out to be rather a damp squib. The hours stretched from quarter-past-nine to one in the afternoon, with an occasional hour later in the afternoon. There were several short-service commission surgeon lieutenants who acted as housemen. We acted as understudies to them on their waiting nights and were attached to a ward to drop in on as we pleased. It was often difficult to avoid the impression that we were simply in the way. In the mess, there were various senior naval specialists whose homes were in the grounds.

A Mess Dinner entailed a different approach to authority from that of Edinburgh Royal. After a good dinner, with plenty of alcohol, there was the usual ribald singing and a raid on the nurses' home. Setting off the fire extinguishers there led to a severe reprimand and a clear warning that 'this was not done in the Service'. This was, however, a very good evening in a place where we had learned the unfamiliar tedium of having too little to do. Trips to London, including visits to *Look Back In Anger* and the new Slade and Reynolds musical *Free As Air* were enjoyable. The real fun at Chatham had nothing to do with medicine. Certainly most of us enjoyed the various 'extra-curricular' activities.

As we had been told in Portsmouth, it was part of the drill for all newcomers to the Navy to learn something of boat handling. We did this by taking a pinnace out on the Medway and taking turns to handle it. The task was certainly not as easy as it appeared, but apparently fulfilled the premise that anyone might be the last man alive on a ship involved in enemy action. On another wintry morning, we were taken to the diving tank. Three of us got into frogman suits with flippers and discovered how easy it was to swim so equipped. We even did a little welding underwater, a task I for one, didn't know was possible.

The 'ABC' course (Atomic, Bacterial and Chemical) involved sniffing mustard gas, and playing with Geiger Counters. One afternoon we went to the Fire Fighting School. Clothed in oilskins and wellies, we attempted to extinguish roaring oil fires set in big trays. The petty officers in charge drove us relentlessly forward into the smoke and flames, in front of an audience of gaping sea cadets. There was a great deal of loud shouting and we found ourselves going much further towards the blaze than seemed safe.

The last and most exciting event at Chatham was the afternoon spent at the Damage Control School. Everyone who goes to sea on one of HM ships has to do this course. The thinking behind it is simple. A ship may be damaged below the waterline by enemy action, or by accident, and it is necessary for those on board to know what action to take. This mock-up of a ship's compartment was very realistic. We again dressed in oilskins and wellies. The ship's compartment, supposedly below the waterline, looked perfectly normal, at first. We had just finished a briefing on the action we were to take when, suddenly, there was a series of loud bangs, and water started pouring in from a three-foot 'shell hole' in the side of the compartment. The lights went out and the water continued to flood in to this enclosed space. There were more loud bangs and flashes, probably from Thunderflashes, which are pretty impressive and used to great effect to induce fear and trembling when required. Water started to flood in from two more simulated 'shell holes'. It was very scary and, although we believed we were being monitored, very realistic. Action was urgently called for and we quickly learned what was meant by 'Damage Control'. Emergency lighting was rigged and, by its feeble illumination, we struggled to plug the holes and stem the flow of water. Already it was above knee height and by now we were wet through and hoarse from shouting.

Several large and heavy wooden beams had been placed in the compartment before the exercise began. With these and a pile of sacking, we fought hard to control the water which continued flooding in at an increasing rate. Things became even worse when a 'water main' burst in the roof, accompanied by another loud bang. The water main had been 'pierced by shrapnel'. The flow of water seemed unstoppable and we became wetter and hoarser as time went by. There was a real feeling of danger, which proved too much for one of our number, who moaned about the cold and wet. He was a man of generous proportions and his complaints were only temporarily silenced when we threatened to use him to plug one of the shell holes. This realistic exercise was the highlight of our stay at Chatham, enjoyed by all who took part – except, perhaps, the fat man.

We now awaited news of our postings amid many rumours, most false as usual. The appointments came through from the Admiralty in dribs and drabs, those of us still waiting becoming more and more anxious as the days dragged by. At last, my posting came through. I was to join the 3rd Frigate Squadron in the Far East as squadron medical officer. It was exactly what I had asked for during my interview and I could not have been more pleased.

3

To the Far East

After I was fitted with tropical uniform and had been inoculated against cholera and typhoid, I went briefly on leave. Then there was a chartered flight to Singapore in a Hermes aircraft, operated by Airwork, which proceeded in several stages, refuelling at Brindisi, Ankara, Basra, Karachi, Delhi, Calcutta and Bangkok. When the flight left from Blackbushe in Hampshire, I found, to my surprise, that I had been appointed Senior Naval Officer, Naval Draft. This was because I had two stripes on my sleeve. The fact that there was a red stripe between them – indicating that I belonged to the medical branch – did not seem to matter. Nor did it matter that there were two sub-lieutenants (SD) on the flight. They were both much older than I was, having been promoted up from the lower deck to the wardroom as a result of their expertise in one or other branch of naval technology. Having risen up the hard way, they were well used to the ways of the Navy. The rest of the passengers were ratings and naval families, some with babies.

To be Senior Naval Officer on this flight was a surprise. I was probably the newest naval recruit on the plane and even the young wives knew more of the workings of the Navy than I did. It was impossible not to feel in the same boat as the politician Lord Carson at the turn of the century, when he had said, 'My only qualification for being put at the head of the Navy is that I am very much at sea.' This was especially the case when I found out I had to leave one of the SD officers behind because the plane was overbooked. This decision was left to me and had to be made quickly as take-off approached. I discussed it with the two men but neither seemed keen to volunteer and eventually I had to decide between them. The man concerned did not like it and I knew how Lord Carson felt.

Brindisi, located on the heel of Italy, was remembered for an excellent meal of pasta. All appeared to be going well until we reached Ankara in Turkey. The pilot had difficulty landing because of low cloud and needed to make a steep descent because of the surrounding mountains. The result was a heavy landing on one wheel and almost a wingtip. This resulted in a bent axle and a week's stay in Ankara, because a replacement wheel and axle had to be flown out from the UK. This unexpected visit to an Asiatic city was a bonus for me, but many of the children were quickly unhappy.

There were some RAF junior ranks on the plane and it fell to me and the senior RAF officer to allocate rooms. As there were seventy-five of us altogether this meant sharing, sometimes with four to a room. While each room had a bath and a WC, the drainage was very slow and there was no hot water. Furthermore, there was no fresh milk and even tinned milk was scarce. Inevitably, all the babies and some of the adults developed diarrhoea and I spent time each day trying to ensure that everyone had the appropriate fluids and some food. This was particularly difficult because of the attitude of the staff from the hotel, the 'Turist Oteli', in the Ataturk Bulvari. Our only contact with the management was through a sinister male receptionist, who looked straight out of a Hollywood gangster film. He wore a green corduroy smoking jacket, had a big moustache and spoke only a little English. Obviously he felt we were a nuisance and we even had difficulty persuading him to give us boiled water. We managed, however, to get a supply of baby food, which had been flown out from the UK on a scheduled flight. I found it ironic that my first patients in the Navy were under one year of age, but the mothers coped very well. The food offered by the hotel was largely flavoured with garlic and there was a plentiful supply of oranges. The other guests included foreign correspondents, here for the Baghdad Pact conference of which more will be said later. We met two British textile experts and there were several Turkish businessmen.

Ankara was an interesting place. The monument to Kamal Ataturk, the founder of modern Turkey and the defender of the Dardanelles against the British in 1915, is located on the city outskirts. Looking out from it, there is a magnificent view of thousands of red and orange roofs against a background of snow-covered mountains. Snow fell intermittently on the yellow muddy streets. The city appeared poor and was quite different from anywhere I had seen in Europe. Occasionally a bank or a business was housed in an ultra-modern building, but these were few and far between. The people appeared downcast and the streets were full of untidy, bored soldiers, wandering about aimlessly, sometimes hand in hand. One man was delighted when I told him I had seen his far smarter troops at the Edinburgh Military Tattoo.

The muddy streets provided employment to many shoeshine boys. Their technique was meticulous and time-consuming, but immediately after leaving them it was impossible to avoid becoming just as muddy as before. Their stands were of polished brass. Tea was a feature of everyday life: on the street and in the office, a circular array of brass cups was carried about on elaborate copper trays. Bread was sold in the late afternoon from street kiosks and was carried unwrapped under arm by men in their working clothes. Glass cases, laid down on the pavement, contained up to a dozen boiled sheep brains. These were sold, steaming, inside the sheep's skull. Many varieties of nut were displayed on trays, as hors d'oeuvres. Having made his choice, the buyer then specified how the nuts were to be cooked, including as a pulp of some kind.

I spent time exploring the city with the SD officer and the RAF man. Evenings provided entertainment as Ankara was, for all its poverty, well provided with nightclubs. We spent one evening at the 'Casinos', which was very smooth and expensive, hosting a cabaret show which lasted for almost an hour. The best known, however, was the Bomanti. This, at the time of our stay in the capital, was the place to see 'Miss Pamela', who had 'taken Turkey and the whole of the Levant by storm'. This, at least, was the verdict of two of the staff of Hugh Foot, a British diplomat attending a Baghdad Pact meeting. The Baghdad Pact was a mutual security organisation guarding against Communism, which involved Turkey, the UK, Pakistan and Iran. Senior British and American diplomats were in town, moving rapidly around the city in processions of fast cars. The two aides slipped in to the Bomanti hurriedly, just before Miss Pamela's second spot of the evening. They were given seats at a table beside ours.

Miss Pamela was, as they say, something else. She was tall with a beautiful face and a superb body. The last was gradually revealed in a striptease act, but the *pièce de résistance* was yet to come. Her striptease over, she turned her attention to the four tassels, which were now, apart from a minimal *cache-sexe*, her only clothing. One tassel was attached to the tip of each breast, one to each buttock. Slowly, after one or two false starts, she managed to set all four in motion. Her aim, which she achieved, was to set up a contrary rotation between the two sets of tassels. Eventually, when all was running smoothly, she bent forward from the waist and moved around the room, turning slowly through three hundred and sixty degrees as she went. On finishing, the applause was thunderous and Turkey undoubtedly remained taken by storm.

By an amazing piece of good fortune, this stunning girl had heard of our plight, stuck as we were in the city. She turned out to be English, her father said to be a vicar in Streatham. She had a car and, before we knew it, the uncomplaining three of us were sitting down to porterhouse steaks, flown in from America, in the American Officers' Club. Perhaps not surprisingly, Miss Pamela had honorary membership of this club, a favour they extended to her guests, remarkably without charge for hospitality or even the food. Miss Pamela was someone we were delighted to meet, on all counts, although it did take us some time to recover.

On the last night before the plane was finally repaired and had been test flown, we went to the Ankara Opera House for a performance of *The Barber of Seville*. The opera house was beautiful, but the reaction of the audience at the end was merely perfunctory. Curtain calls and the national anthem were completed at breakneck speed and the audience seemed in a great hurry to leave.

Next day everyone was glad to resume the journey. We flew first to Basra and then to Karachi, where there was a planned overnight stay at Miniwalla's Grand Palace Hotel. This was an airy place outside the city, very different from Ankara. I slept under a mosquito net for the first time and had a shirt washed and ironed in three hours by the cabin steward. In the evening we went around Karachi by taxi. The driver's little brother, for whom there was no room, bumped about in the boot. When we disembarked, the driver followed us around on foot, making sure he got his pay. Our impression of Karachi was of vast numbers of people, heat and squalor. Camels paced about, people slept on makeshift beds on the covered pavements, and an old man defaecated quite openly at one street junction. It was a relief to leave the poverty-stricken place.

It was, however, exciting to have a clear view of the western Himalayas on the way to Delhi, although this was not the Everest group. We continued on to Calcutta. Shortly after take-off, as evening fell, we had a fine view of the many mouths of the Ganges. Bangkok by night was just a little too much for the tired children on the plane. They gave us an excellent meal on the flight, but it was a relief to all when we touched down at Paya Lebar in Singapore.

So far, Naval medicine was not at all what I had expected and I was pleased to see the families depart for their new homes. Little did I know, however, that I was to meet one or two of them again, when I was briefly ashore and roped in to do a night on the 'medical guard' roster.

4

Singapore

While it was a relief to finish a long flight, it was a shock to walk out of the plane at Paya Lebar into a wall of heat. And, it was still only early morning. The flight had been full of interest, but the change to the humid heat of Singapore took me by surprise. In a short space of time, the world had changed yet again, to one as different from Ankara as Ankara had been from Edinburgh.

Why, in any case, had it been necessary to fly half-way around the world to join a Royal Navy ship? The answer lies with Sir Stamford Raffles. This man, who had been the British East India Company administrator, had signed a treaty with the Sultan of Johore in 1819, which led to Singapore becoming the centre of British colonial activity in Southeast Asia. The treaty had not specifically given ownership of the island to Britain, but it was formally acquired in 1867, when it became a British Crown Colony. In effect Raffles had 'seized' Singapore for Britain without instructions from London, but such was the power of Britain at that time that ownership by default went unchallenged. After World War I, the British built a large naval base on the north end of the island and thereafter commanded one of the world's busiest shipping and trade routes: the sixty-five mile long Singapore Strait. Apart from a miserable period in World War II, when the island was captured by the Japanese, the greatly enlarged British Far East Fleet had been based between Singapore and Hong Kong. This was the fleet to which the 3rd Frigate Squadron, the squadron I was to join, belonged.

Heat I had expected, but the intensity of the light and, in particular, the degree of humidity proved exhausting. I felt glad that I was to be at sea shortly, where I hoped it would be cooler. As quickly as was possible, I changed from clothes suitable for a British winter to a lightweight, white uniform.

The British Naval Base on Singapore Island was on HMS *Terror*, a stone frigate. The officers' mess resembled a first-class country hotel and was designed for a hot climate. The building was wide-eaved to produce maximum shade and was painted white throughout. Punkah fans whirred overhead and the whole structure was spacious and open to the air. Armchairs were of cane and the floors were uncarpeted. The bedrooms, or 'cabins', were fitted with 'Western Saloon'-type doors, that is spring-loaded half-doors which met in the middle, enabling air to circulate. The beds were fitted with mosquito nets, hung from a thin, four-poster frame. Clothes left in a wardrobe quickly became covered in mildew, in spite of the fact that a lamp was left burning beside them at all times. Breakfast, often started off with pomelo and usually followed by bacon and egg, was eaten in a beautiful room, open on two sides. This provided a splendid view of the Straits of Johore, on the edge of which *Terror* was built. The Straits were so narrow that we were close to the tropical vegetation of Malaya's Johore province. Singapore lies off the foot of Malaya and is connected to it by a causeway. Malaya was out of bounds to British personnel, but at the end of my time in the Far East, I learned the hard way that this restriction was not always obeyed. The naval dockyard, which I was shortly to see, was a short car journey away. The huge international port and town of Singapore was eleven miles away, on the south coast of the island.

For those permanently based at *Terror*, life was comfortable. The food was excellent and editions of British newspapers were available by airmail. Sports facilities included a large swimming pool. I spent a long time wondering what the large white wooden object in the grounds was, before realising it was the outdoor cinema screen. Sunday cinema was an important highlight of the week, at which the tropical mess kit of the officers, and the evening dresses of their ladies, added to the feeling of a country club. We

HMS Terror, Singapore

lived life out of doors as much as possible, at least until the monsoon season arrived. Then the huge ditches of concrete, or 'monsoon drains', were quickly filled with the rain, which lashed down with great intensity. Mosquitoes were more prevalent in this weather and the mosquito net on my bed was most welcome. The high humidity made it difficult for sweat to evaporate, so one always felt sticky.

On the Equator, darkness falls year round at six in the afternoon, after which there is an insistent loud chirping of cicadas. At night in the wet season, I lay behind my 'bed net' and listened to the rain thundering down, while the half-height, double doors of my cabin creaked as they swung in the wind.

The white tropical uniform was a boon in these surroundings. Even watch straps could be made from expendable white cotton, an example of the cheap and lightweight clothing available from local Chinese tailors. A few of these industrious individuals were allowed into the base to solicit trade. Sea island cotton shirts, made to measure in two days, cost very little and it took only a week to have a lightweight suit made to measure.

The first medicine-related job I had in the Far East was not too taxing. It involved attending a boxing competition between the Navy and the Royal Army Service Corps. I had to examine the boxers before their bouts and decide on their fitness to continue, if it seemed as if one or other was taking too much punishment. On this occasion, there were no problems.

After a few days of hedonistic acclimatisation, I joined the 3rd Frigate Squadron. Life was again about to change. The man I was to relieve as medical officer, 3rd Frigate Squadron, or 'MO3' to use the shorthand title, was at sea when I arrived, his ship undertaking six days of gunnery practice. He left me a message saying, 'Contact me on recovery.' This was a stroke of good luck, as acclimatisation to life in Singapore was taking some time. I had time for some sight-seeing in the town of Singapore and, in particular, to the Tiger Balm Gardens. This remarkable place was founded, as was the cure-all Tiger Balm, by a man called Aw Boon Haw. This made his fortune. It was a combination of cleverness and horror, with everything in bright colours, consisting mainly of three-dimensional sculptures depicting scenes from Chinese religion and mythology. One bas-relief, for example, was of the 'Three Executors of the Court of Hell'.

The time had now come to join HMS *Crane*, the only ship of the 3rd Frigate Squadron to be in harbour at the time. She had recently arrived, having only just finished her gunnery practice. I met her medical officer, who I have mentioned earlier, a lugubrious fellow Scot who seemed only too glad to hand over the reins to me and return home. For the beginning of a new job, this was somewhat daunting, but I quickly realised he had always been an apparently miserable chap, and that he was alone in his gloom. He did, however, give me some useful advice, mostly medical, but I had to quickly learn the way in which the day was organised on a frigate.

In spite of the careful introduction we had to naval ways at Portsmouth, the method by which the day is regulated on a warship was not mentioned. I therefore had to learn it when I arrived on board for the first time, although, to a squadron officer such as myself, most of the regulations did not apply. The learning process, however, did not prove difficult. The system employed depended upon a series of loudspeaker announcements, or 'pipes'. These were broadcast throughout the ship and, while some were self-explanatory, the meaning of others had to be learned. The following are examples of each:

Call the hands! Call the hands! Call the hands! You've had your time, now I want mine! Don't turn over, turn out! [A wakeup call, first thing in the morning.]

Both watches of the hands fall in on the quarterdeck! [Shortened in conversation] to 'Both watches ... ! [At start of the day's work. The ship's company was divided into port and starboard watches.]

Morning watchmen join up part of ship! [The men who 'had had the Morning' i.e. had been on watch from 4am to 8am, were given time off before starting their day's work.]

Stand easy! [Morning and afternoon break in work of the ship.]

Out pipes! Hands carry on with your work! [End of stand easy.]

Captain's (or First Lieutenant's) requestmen and defaulters to clean! [Those who wanted, or had, to see the captain or first lieutenant were required to change from their working clothes into the correct uniform, with appropriate smartness of appearance.]

Men under punishment and stoppage of leave to muster

Hands fall in for entering (or leaving) harbour! Hands out of the rig of the day clear off the upper deck! [The emphasis was again on smartness of appearance. Some men, e.g. the bow and stern rope handling parties, had prescribed positions to occupy.]

Special sea duty men close up! Cox'n on the wheel! [The more experienced men were brought into service for more demanding tasks e.g. entering or leaving harbour.]

Special sea duty navigation party close up. Cable party not required! [For example when going through a narrows, such as the Johore Strait or at some places in the Japanese Inland Sea. Note the difference from 'Special sea duty men.]

Hands to tea, supper! etc.

Pipe down! [Lights out.]

Junior rates pipe down! [Younger ratings lights out.]

Hands to make and mend clothes! [A 'make and mend' or half-day. Usually greeted by a cheer.]

Libertymen fall in abreast the brow! [Those going ashore muster at the gangway.]

Free gangway is now open (or closed)! [Anyone off watch can go ashore.]

Hands shift into night clothing! [When working in hours of darkness.]

Shut all screen doors and scuttles! [For watertight integrity.]

Assume Damage Control State 1! [When action imminent.]

Assume Damage Control State 3! [When manoeuvring in harbour.]

Crash darken ship! [When action imminent.]

Clear up mess decks and flats for rounds! [Followed by] Stand by for rounds!

'Rounds' are a weekly feature of life on a frigate. The captain leads an inspecting party, including the medical officer, around the living areas looking for untidiness and lack of hygiene. The punishments for breaches of order may be severe, and the stratagems employed for avoiding detection of such breaches were often ingenious. All men on such a small ship have to live as best they can among a mass of often noisy machinery. The lucky ones find room to sling a hammock. It is surprising that in such an environment, also possessing a lack of air conditioning, captain's rounds seldom uncovered serious problems. This was a good indication of the state of morale on board the ship.

The following are some pipes associated with gun actions and drills:

Hands to emergency/shelter stations! [The latter involved protection against radiation.]

Ammunition supply parties close up!

Policy, surface! Four inch stand to! Director target! Director on! Four inch target! Four inch engage! Stop loading, stop loading, stop loading! Cease firing, cease firing, cease firing! Four inch relax! Four inch train fore and aft! Four inch sponge out! [These pipes are all as heard, but may not be in the correct order. The ships in the squadron mounted four or six four-inch guns. They fired either singly or all together as broadsides. The latter made a satisfactory noise.]

Cover guns! [Said with a pause between the two words. At 18:00 or in bad weather.]

Alarm aircraft starboard (say)! [Followed quickly by] Aircraft bearing green ninety (say) Close range, engage! [This was followed in practice air attacks by a most satisfactory din as the ship's lighter armament opened up. These guns fired 'break up shot', that is plastic rounds which broke up just after they left the barrel, but gave the gunner a feeling of firing the real thing.]

Some pipes, among a large number, associated with boat chills:

Away sea boat's (or motorboat's) crew! Lower away! Out pins! Slip!Man the falls! Many the falls! Hoist away! Vast heaving! Hoist away inboard (or outboard) fall! Separate the falls! Ease to lifelines! Turn in motorboat (or whaler)!

Other pipes:

Up spirits! Leading hands of messes muster for rum. [Tot time' or rum issue. This took place at midday and preceded lunch. Junior rates were given 'grog', i.e. watered down rum, instead of full strength. The ritual associated with the supply of tots, and the consumption thereof is elaborate. Some reference to it will be found later.]

D'ye hear there? [Usually used by the Captain when speaking unexpectedly on the ship's broadcast. The US Navy's equivalent is 'Now hear this!]

5

Joining HMS *Crane*

My arrival on board a real frigate, as opposed to one of the stone variety such as *Victory* at Portsmouth and *Terror* at Singapore, was not auspicious. Having crossed the brow, or gangway, I remembered, as I was taught at Portsmouth, to salute the quarterdeck. This is one of the Navy's traditions, beginning during medieval times when a religious shrine was set up on the quarterdeck of every British warship. It was considered correct to remove one's hat when passing, which was replaced by saluting when boarding the vessel. So far so good and I felt quite pleased with myself. Suddenly, however, I was confronted by a commander, who came smartly to attention and saluted. I realized too late that I should have saluted him first, considering he had three stripes on his shoulder to my two. The problems that had manifested at Portsmouth were clearly not yet resolved. Not only was he a commander, but he was *Crane's* commanding officer. He turned out to be an amiable man and, after polite chat in a clipped manner, he arranged for someone to show me around the ship.

The pleasure of being on a Royal Navy ship was tempered by the realisation that this was a very different world. To begin with, the variety of broad English accents, of which there were many, were often difficult to understand. For example, I found *Crane's* coxswain, who was from somewhere in London, completely unintelligible, both at the time and later. Cornish and other West Country accents seemed to predominate, sounding somehow appropriate on the ship's broadcast, although still difficult to understand. Everyone seemed to be very busy as departure for the west coast of Malaya was imminent, and these problems soon disappeared. I found the SBA, or sick berth attendant, busy checking stores. Each frigate possessed an SBA, who were referred to by all as 'the doctor'. He was so called even when I was being addressed. 'The doctor said so and so … ,' the men would explain to me. I was known as 'the medical officer'.

It was from this SBA that I learned how a naval sickbay operated and how it differed from civilian medical practice. For a start, the majority of the patients were basically healthy men, which meant that there was little work to be done. This being the Navy and this being the Far East, the predominant reason for attendance at the sickbay was venereal disease (VD).

The incidence of VD was astonishingly high on all ships, in spite of the strong emphasis on prevention. Lectures were given, pamphlets circulated, and free condoms made available – a box at the gangway bearing the message, 'Take one for your friend.' The SBA explained to me the casual attitude which many men adopted towards VD, and I was glad to be handed the good notes compiled by my predecessor in the squadron. These were accompanied by a Fleet Order, issued from a great height but very useful. This discussed both diagnosis and treatment.

Gonorrhoea was the commonest disease in Singapore and Malaya, but it came second to NSU, or non-specific urethritis, in Hong Kong and Japan. The latter was of two main types, the treatment for each being detailed in the notes. This was very important because the diseases were unfamiliar to one who had just arrived from the UK. Important also was the 'test of cure', which required careful organisation because of frequent re-infections, the movement of men and medical facilities. One of the main aims of management was to avoid masking the much more serious syphilis, which was happily, and surprisingly, not too common a disease in the Far East.

Other diseases encountered were, apparently, much as in Britain, but there was a high incidence of 'Singapore Ear' or otitis externa. Overall, minor trauma and VD were the two commonest reasons for attendance at the sickbay.

I opened one of the sickbay cupboards and, to my great surprise, I found a pair of obstetrical forceps. These were indeed on the stores list and were a reminder that Royal Navy ships were sometimes called to assist the civilian population during various emergencies. By now, I had at least begun to understand my new job, and I found my way to the wardroom. Officers lived right aft in cabins opening on to a cramped area, surrounding the wardroom itself. The latter served as living and dining area. On a ship as small as a frigate, only the senior officers – the first lieutenant, the engineer officer and the navigator – had single cabins. The rest had to share. As a squadron officer, I had no fixed abode, and this meant I had to sleep where I could. My first 'half-cabin' was shared with the 'gunner', an SD officer, who accepted my invasion of his space without protest. His cabin was small even for one man, and my bed was the backrest of his couch, raised horizontally at night. The number of cabins do not allow for extra bodies, so I got used to captains' emergency sea cabins and a half-cabin here and there. This applied, of course, to all squadron officers. These officers included those sent to check on the efficiency of each department, so their presence was not always too welcome in any case. Ironically, one of the medical officer's responsibilities was to report on the habitability of each compartment in the ship.

There were five ships in the 3rd Frigate Squadron, but, as they usually operated independently, I was nearly always on board *Crane, Modeste* or *St Brides Bay.* There were, in fact, two doctors in the squadron, but, because of the independence of operations and the size of the area, I only met the other man once, and, then, only briefly. The other ships were *Cardigan Bay* and the Royal New Zealand Navy's frigate *Rotoiti.* The ships were all much the same, being mostly of the modified Black Swan class and displacing fifteen hundred tons. *Modeste* had the pennant number U42 and was known as 'The Fighting Forty Two', or 'The Mighty Mo'.

Getting used to life in the wardroom proved easy. The first, and lasting, impression was of the intensity and liveliness of the conversation. So much so in one case, that the wardroom had a wooden paddle mounted on a varnished board that hung on the wall, or 'bulkhead'. On the board was painted 'The Paddle Club', and the token ownership of the paddle was given to the man who had succeeded in 'stirring it up' most in any given argument. Sometimes these arguments were fierce, but most were in good humour. The topics ranged from world politics to the daily running of the ship.

The fact that I was a national serviceman thrown into the company of highly trained professional naval people proved completely irrelevant, for which I was grateful. This, however, was not the case for a fellow medic from Edinburgh who was stationed on a cruiser, also located in the Far East. In spite of having a large single cabin, a lieutenant (D) or dentist, also known as a 'toothwright' or 'toothie' in the Navy, and a surgeon captain on the ship to carry all the cans, he was not happy. 'Too much bull!' he said, meaning too much formality. This was not the case with frigates, where the opposite was often the rule, although discipline was rigidly maintained.

When I took my first sick parade, I found I had to get used to the language. One man came to me and said 'I've reason to believe I've got CDA, sir'. This means VD, but nobody knew what CDA stood for. Anti-malarial pills had to be distributed and the stores were in a mess. One useful trick in this situation was to employ the phrase, 'Lost at sea in heavy weather', which could be used for anything missing from the inventory and, indeed, many things were. This was a well-known trick, however, and could not be used too often. I quickly found that the medical officer's report for this ship, a quarterly requirement, was due. Because many of the stores were, to my eye, old fashioned and ineffective, I took the chance to say so. The obstetrical forceps were present and their use has already been mentioned. But what use was there, I asked in full declamatory style, for such remedies as Pil.. Colch. et Hyoscy., Oil of Eucalyptus and Tabs. Ferri. Sulphus. cum Manganese et Copper? These and other outdated medicines were still part of the standard medical chest, although the much used antibiotic Aureomycin was in short supply. In addition, the day of the Latin tag was past.

The island of Singapore lay at the foot of the Malay peninsula to which it was attached by a causeway, as has already been mentioned. The causeway closed the Johore Strait to the westward for ships leaving the Royal Navy's dockyard on the island's north shore. As the causeway crossed the Strait near its western end, all ships wishing to travel west are first required to make a long passage eastwards to the open sea.

It was along this narrow strait that I first went to sea on a RN ship. The scenery, and particularly the smells of the Johore jungle on the port side, were striking, contrasting with the more civilised Singapore Island opposite. Arriving at Johore Shoal Buoy at the end of the Strait, the ships turned south, rounded Singapore Island and then headed north and west into the Malacca Strait. The Malacca Strait lies between Malaya and Sumatra. The sweet smell of decaying vegetation was coming out from the Malayan shore and accompanied us all the way up to Penang, our destination. Our trip was a 'half-jolly' – a trip which was half work, half pleasure.

Penang lies 400 miles north of Singapore and, though the 'capital' is Georgetown, the whole place is known as Penang. It was the first of Britain's 'Straits Settlements' founded in 1867. Together with Singapore and Malacca, these represented our attempts in the region to add to the British Empire, but the Settlements were 'dissolved' in 1946. Penang was essentially Chinese in population and character, and did not prove particularly interesting to visiting ships. It was a mixture of the rich and the poor, with rickshaws sharing the

Open air barbers in Penang

untidy streets with modem cars including the odd MG. HMS *Crane* had been 'working up', getting all its departments working as well as possible, for some months and was due for a break. It was, therefore, a pity that this place had little to offer us, but the unusual shops did yield many 'rabbits', as souvenirs are known. During our stay, I was, for a time, the duty medical officer for all visiting Royal Navy. ships. The ship, and not the medic, is said to be 'medical guard' on these occasions, and indicates this by flying the appropriate small flag. This has a white diagonal cross on a navy background, exactly the same as a Scottish saltire. Each ship can thus see where the doctor is to be found. As we were all at anchor, movement from ship to ship was by motorboat, but the visitors stayed healthy.

As noted, Penang did not have much to offer. We therefore had to make what we could of it, and I started by meeting a *muezzin*. He told me that, in addition to being the *muezzin* he was second priest in his mosque, and he invited me to climb his minaret to see the impressive electronic equipment he used to tell the faithful of the hours of prayer. We were later invited to the Penang Sports Club for a dinner and dance by a slightly zany Chinese businessman. The dance proved a bit of a washout, as there were said to be only seven white women over the age of fifteen on the island. The meal, however, was very good, served in the Chinese style with multiple dishes of tasty food from which one helped oneself. They included shark's fin soup, sweet and sour something, fried rice and prawns, and small birds cooked with their heads still on. On the way back to the ship, we heard some very good Anglo/Chinese pop music coming from a shop. Attempts to find out what this was were met by the reply, 'This is a ladies' tailor,' which wasn't very helpful. We made a bit of a boob on the way back to the jetty, meeting the captain waiting for the same boat. Unfortunately we arrived in trishaws which we were forbidden to use. Luckily for us, however, the captain looked the other way.

The return journey to Singapore was again in flat calm. The full moon over the sea, the smell of land as before, and the occasional lights on the coast of Sumatra meant, as they say, I was 'glad I had joined'.

On the return to *Terror*, I did a stint as medical guard, the small saltire flying from *Crane*. Twice I was called to the Asian Hospital, which caters for

Asian dockyard workers and their families. On the first visit, I saw an old chap with pneumonia, and on the second, a woman whose family had brought her in because 'she wouldn't stop crying'. I did not find out why this was the case, and the presence of an interpreter failed to resolve the issue. In the male ward, there were three rows of men, all lying in bed as if on parade – all stripped to the waist and wearing turbans. Many people in this small hospital had TB, a common disease in the area. Men on the frigates, living as they did in a confined space, had therefore to have chest X-rays every six months. One of my predecessors contracted the disease right at the end of his time on these ships.

Shortly after we returned from Penang, there was 'almost' an emergency. The Fleet was brought to four hours readiness for sea in response to bombings in Sumatra. The 3rd Frigate Squadron's *Modeste* was to be among the first ships to cross the Malacca Strait and I had to be ready to join her. Nothing happened in the end and we subsequently joined the rest of the fleet for Exercise Fotex. This was held off the beautiful island of Tioman, on the east side of Malaya, and was under the command of an admiral. The sea there was very clear which allowed us to see numerous sea snakes. These, however, were not a pretty sight.

The exercise known as Fotex produced a small medical drama. The SBA on *Modeste* thought he had a rating with appendicitis. I was summoned to *Crane's* bridge by the Captain 'F', the man in charge of all the frigates in the squadron. My request to go across and see the man was refused twice by the admiral, in spite of warnings of the risk of untreated appendicitis. I think this was on the grounds that we were due in port in twenty-four hours. Very much as a second best option, I decided to prescribe penicillin and streptomycin. Communication with *Modeste* was, for some reason, by Aldis lamp only, and the receiving signalman had great difficulty with the word 'streptomycin'. Time and again he flashed back, 'Please repeat words after penicillin.' I saw the man when we returned and was quite happy that he did not have appendicitis. Two points occurred to me, however. Would the admiral have been quite so casual if we were not due in so soon? And, as he was on a cruiser with two doctors to advise him, did he really need my opinion? For a moment, but only a moment, I wondered if the exercise on which we had embarked included testing the new medical officer. This seemed an ignoble thought but I did wonder!

After Fotex, we went to sea again to carry out gunnery shoots, amongst other things. It was then that I realised that spare bodies on frigates were quickly put to use. The usual opening remark was 'Doc! You've nothing to do. Would you … ?' First I was co-opted into the ship's crypto team. Signals and replies were received in code. With the aid of a special kind of typewriter, the meaningless groups of letters were typed by a signalman on a long thin strip of paper. This must have been soul-destroying. Only an officer with a code book was allowed to translate these groups into plain English. The opposite, of course, applied on outgoing messages. I found this job interesting, but the second job which I was roped in to do was much more exciting. The opening remark was again 'Doc! You've nothing to do. Would you … etc?' This time the gunnery officer asked me to be the fall-of-shot recorder in a four-inch shoot. The target was a Battle Practice Target, or BPT. This was a wooden frame on floats, towed behind a tug on a long cable. The ship's main armament of six four-inch guns was to fire broadsides at this target, a broadside being a simultaneous firing of all six. The fall-of-shot recorder sat beside the gunnery officer high up above the bridge, while the turrets went through their full broadside firing drill. The warning clang of the firing gongs was immediately followed by a deafening crash as the six guns fired. The ship lurched and the smoke cleared just in time for me to see and report the fall of shot. Good shooting was a 'straddle', for example, 'Two short, four over!' Appropriate adjustments were made in each turret until straddles were usual. The accuracy obtained depended, to a large extent, on the order to fire being given at exactly the right moment. This was the gunnery officer's job. He had to allow, amongst other things which I did not understand, for the roll of the ship. As might be expected, anything landing too near the tug was greeted by an unprintable outburst from her skipper, heard all over our ship courtesy of the ship-to-ship broadcast. This shoot was great fun, as was the next exercise which involved the anti-aircraft guns, mainly Bofors and Oerlikons.

The Royal Air Force, based at Changi on Singapore Island, flew their fast fighter jets at us. They peeled off in sequence at height, as in American films, and levelled themselves just over the waves. Lining us up, they came straight towards us one after another, pulling up over our mast at the very last moment. I stood behind one of the guns as the gunner fired close-range 'breakup' ammunition at the planes. As mentioned previously, these rounds break up but give a realistic feeling to the gunners and the onlookers. The last minute diversions of the jets, which appeared to vie with each another as to who could come closest to the tip of the mast, were very exciting. The clatter of every gun that would bear added to the drama..

On return to harbour, I went into the town of Singapore again. There was one modern shopping centre and a handful of beautiful new buildings. A man recognised the EU Athletic Club tie I was wearing. He turned out to be a friend of my sister, who was training to be a teacher in Edinburgh at the time. The word got out that *Crane* was shortly to go north to Hong Kong, the Royal Navy's other Far Eastern base. By all accounts this was quite a place, but our arrival there was delayed by the unusual events described in the following chapter.

6

An unexpected diversion

All of us in *Crane's* wardroom to which, despite being a squadron officer of no fixed abode, I now felt I belonged, were looking forward to the fleshpots of Hong Kong. The wardroom consisted of the first lieutenant, a lieutenant commander, the engineer officer, the navigating officer ('Pilot', 'Vasco'), the gunnery officer, the TAS officer (a torpedo and anti-submarine specialist), the gunner (a commissioned chief petty officer who wore the single stripe of the 'lieutenant SD'), the electrical officer and two ex-Dartmouth sub-lieutenants under training. In addition, we carried a constructor lieutenant on this trip, who had finished a Cambridge BSc and was doing a year's sea time to complete his training as a Naval ship designer. He had one amazing characteristic: his response to beer, which we discovered on a recent 'run ashore'. Normally, people start an evening bright and cheerful and get a little sleepy as the evening progresses. He did exactly the opposite, which was a difficult situation for the rest of us. Perhaps this only applies in relation to the local Tiger beer, but somehow I doubt it. For a time we also carried a 'Schoolie', or instructor lieutenant, who is really a school master. It followed that the wardroom and all available spaces were pretty crowded. The instructor lieutenant had to sleep on a camp bed in the ship's office. As this was unstable with the movement of the ship and as the office had linoleum on the floor, he had to lash his bed to a radiator. It was just as well that I had to leave them suddenly and unexpectedly.

So we were all set for Hong Kong. *Crane* had Captain F on board and we had sailed in company with *Modeste*. These ships, incidentally, are identical to *Amethyst*. This ship became famous and entered the reference books in 1949. Commanded by Lieutenant Commander Kerans, she was trapped by the Communists in the Yangtze River, after being in action against them. She made her escape in a gallant hundred and thirty mile dash down the river, reaching the sea intact. Our passage to Hong Kong proceeded uneventfully through the South China Sea until we were passing the entrance to the Gulf of Siam. A signal from London was then received by 'F'. It had been reported that the Indonesians had been interfering with British merchant shipping off the coast of Borneo, and Captain F was ordered to detach one ship to go at once to Tawau, on the border between British North Borneo and Indonesian Borneo.

'F' decided that *Modeste* should go. I first heard of this as I was sitting in the *Crane*'s wardroom after lunch and the phone from the bridge rang. 'F' wasted no words. 'Doc, I'm sending *Modeste* off to Borneo to investigate some trouble with the Indonesians. I want you to go with her. She's coming alongside now. Be ready to transfer to her in ten minutes.' A quick glance through the scuttle (porthole) confirmed her imminent arrival, and I had a big rush getting my gear together. Then *Modeste* was travelling close alongside, and I went over to her by jackstay. Immediately she set off to cover the eleven hundred miles to Tawau, by way of the South China and Sulu Seas.

The jackstay transfer had been quickly executed, although the fact that 'F' was watching probably helped. This is the Navy's method of transferring a man or a small quantity of urgent supplies between two ships while at sea. The two ships travel close together at a constant speed and on a constant course. This requires great concentration by the helmsman on each ship. In this case they seemed to travel fast, but it was important that they kept steerage way. The GI (gunnery instructor) of *Crane* fired a Coston gun line across to *Modeste*. This was a light rope attached to a projectile, fired from a special hand-held gun. The rope was caught and a system involving a stronger rope with a travelling pulley on it was then pulled over. From the pulley there dangled a seven foot length of rope with a stirrup at its bottom end. The stirrup was much too wide for a normal foot but I was instructed to place one foot in it and cover the toes with the other foot on the other side. Finally, a loose loop of rope was placed around my shoulders and an inflatable lifejacket around my neck. 'Do NOT blow this up,' the GI ordered. 'If you do, and then fall in, the force of hitting the sea will break your neck. Blow it up as soon as you are in the water.'

The power for the transfer was provided by six men on *Modeste's* deck, just like a tug of a war team. First they raised the pulley and its load, which was me, clear of obstructions, and then ran down the deck towards the stern pulling me over the gap between the ships. It was interesting to note that this method of transfer between moving ships had a built-in failsafe. The end of the rope on which the pulley travelled was not made fast. Instead, it was held in the hands of the men who provided the motive power. This meant that there was always some slack in the system to allow for the inevitable deviation from the common course, no matter how committed the helmsmen was. As quiet as the sea was and although the jackstay was rigged in the bows, I and my rucksack, which came across after me, got pretty wet. Happily, we had not changed from the thin tropical uniform of Singapore to the thicker blue uniform worn during that season in Hong Kong. This meant that de-salting the uniform was not a problem. I received a great welcome from *Modeste's* wardroom, even though I had not met them before, and one guy had to share his cabin with me. Two days later, instead of watching others, I went to work in earnest.

The entire episode, from a quiet after-lunch snooze in one wardroom to getting used to a different frigate which, when travelling at speed rolled about like a demented duck, had taken about a quarter of an hour. Any ideas about having a great time in Hong Kong faded and tentative thoughts of a subsequent Japanese cruise vanished. Borneo, however, sounded more exotic still. The ship's company on *Modeste*, like the wardroom on the *Crane*, had been looking forward to Hong Kong. But the idea that we were to do something proactive and out of the ordinary in Borneo, meant that the ship was buzzing. All departments were ordered to check that they were ready for action and it was during one of these drills, two days later, that an accident befell a chief ordnance artificer.

This man was working on a magazine, low in the ship, when he caught his arm in a shell hoist. He managed to climb a series of vertical ladders and arrived at the sick bay, where he then collapsed. This was a similar reaction to that expected of a soldier who had sustained a major wound in the heat of action. Such a man is so 'fired up' that he can continue fighting for a few moments before collapsing. Climbing those vertical ladders was difficult enough when in tip-top shape. When I saw him, a few minutes later, he had gone into shock, a condition which requires rapid treatment. I set up an intravenous drip and, having cut away his sleeve, got to work on controlling the profuse bleeding. He had sustained a partial traumatic amputation of his left hand. There were several comminuted fractures of the radius and ulna, comminuted meaning that there were several fragments of bone. At first I thought I would have to complete the amputation, but a proper look showed that his radial artery and the main nerves were intact. This made the situation a different proposition. It meant that there might be a chance of saving his hand, if proper reconstructive surgery could be carried out. As we were at this time in the middle of the South China Sea and thus many hours from civilisation, the chances of obtaining such surgery seemed, at best, unlikely.

Once the bleeding had been controlled and his shock lessened, I carried out a proper exploration of the wound. At this point, I was grateful to the ship's SBA, who had an adequate stock of sterile dressings ready, and who sterilised the necessary instruments quickly. I gave the injured man a big dose of morphia, there being no anaesthetic facilities on these ships. As I was about to begin the exploration of the wound there was a knock on the surgery door. The bridge messenger came in and announced, 'From the Captain, sir. The ship is altering course in ten minutes and is expected to roll.' Even though, at that moment I was concentrating on the best way to proceed surgically, I found this funny. Not only was the message typical of the drama-loving captain, but *Modeste* was already rolling quite heavily as she headed for Tawau at her best speed. These little ships were lively in any kind of sea and, indeed, were often unsteady alongside the wall. So the idea that the delicate work of the surgeon would be upset by a further change in sea conditions was comical. The situation seemed straight out of old-fashioned boys' fiction, *Stirring Tales of the Sea* or something similar. I cleaned up the wound, tied off the remaining bleeding points and took out bits of heavily oil-contaminated bone. After applying a firm bandage and elevating the arm on an immobilising splint, I left him reasonably comfortable and went up to the bridge to see the captain.

The *Far East Station Guide Book* listed a well-equipped hospital, called the Duchess of Kent Hospital no less, with European doctors and sisters at Sandakan, on the north coast of Borneo. This was considerably out of our way, but the captain decided to land the man there. The engine room, already operating nearly flat out, was asked to find another two knots. It took sixteen hours to get to Borneo and, in spite of the pitching and rolling, the COA remained quite comfortable with repeated doses of morphia.

The approach to Sandakan is via a narrow and overlooked gorge, which we negotiated carefully in the dark. Because of the uncertainty of the Indonesian situation and the effect that the sudden appearance of a warship on a dark night might have, the captain ordered a large Union Jack to be flown and kept illuminated with an Aldis lamp. We arrived at three in the morning and the man was taken ashore in the motorboat, with the rain driving down. I went with him and met the doctor, who came down to the jetty in an ambulance. The notes of what had been done so far were handed over to him, but unfortunately there was no time to stay longer and we left at once for Tawau.

At Tawau, we stayed at anchor, there being no appropriate jetty to tie up to. Awnings were spread along the length of the ship and were very welcome in the baking heat. This part of Borneo is very isolated, as there is no access to the Tawau area except by sea. The political situation had calmed down after Britain had made the appropriate noises to the Indonesians, but we were asked to reinforce this by patrolling around the area of the troubles. We therefore made a great show of our six four-inch guns and the White Ensign. Creeping up on the echoes which showed up on our radar, we illuminated them suddenly with the big Aldis lamp. Mostly, these turned out to be innocent fishermen, but one night we thought we really had something. Unfortunately, it turned out to be only a fish pole trap, an erection which depends on the tides, as seen in many such areas. We had come a great distance to find nothing in the way of hostile behaviour, but perhaps our very presence was enough to calm things down. We liked to think that this was so, in any case.

Modeste *at Tawau, North Borneo (on the border of British and Indonesian Borneo), with awnings spread against the heat*

Our primary task being quickly over, I could concentrate on one of the secondary responsibilities of a RN ship's doctor. This was to note the medical facilities available in remote places. Eventually this information would find its way into the *Far East Guide Book* as had happened in the South China Sea, leading to the satisfactory diversion to Sandakan. Listing the medical facilities available was a task I genuinely enjoyed. It meant plenty of 'runs ashore' and, to be honest, holiday-like time. At Tawau, there was a small British Colonial Service hospital run by one doctor, working on his own. He was British, 36 years old and responsible for a huge area in which there were fourteen thousand people. I spent the afternoon with him and he told me that he had, just that morning, been repairing a male patient's ruptured urethra, a very difficult operation which, I would have thought, was impossible for a single person to carry out. He said 'I had Hamilton Bailey's *Emergency Surgery* in one hand, and the tools in the other.' How he managed to administer anaesthesia I was uncertain, but I shortly was to meet another medic, working for a timber company. Although I did not confirm this, it seems probable that he would assist the Tawau man on occasion, such as may have taken place during this morning's operation.

There is only one FRCS in the whole of British North Borneo, although we heard on arrival at Tawau that he had sent our injured man straight on to Singapore. From there, the COA was put immediately on a Comet to the UK. Just before we left Borneo, we heard that he had undergone orthopaedic and plastic surgery, and that they hoped to save his hand. This was good news as it meant that the Navy could still employ him in some capacity. This in turn meant that his final pension on leaving the Service would be better.

The Tawau hospital was fascinating. Small and built from wood, its construction sought to enhance any air circulation: window spaces were large and open. There were many cases of malaria, kala-azar and TB in the region. Kala-azar was initially just a name in a text book to me. I learned that it is also known as visceral leishmaniasis and is spread by a type of sand fly. Leprosy was not particularly common in the area, but they did happen to have several cases in the hospital when I was there. There was also a separate maternity unit. The mothers in the postnatal section had white cotton bands around their heads, a local custom which is supposed 'to keep the air out of the baby'. As we walked around we were gazed upon by a group of shackled convicts on the street outside. They were ambling along in the heat, in the charge of policemen who were getting them to knock down coconuts with ultra-long bamboo poles.

The hospitality of the afternoon left me feeling a little limp, and it was to be repeated on another day when we visited a sawmill, eighteen miles up river from Tawau at a place called Wallace Bay. This was run by the Bombay Burma Trading Company. Fourteen British people ran the mill, handling teak and other tropical hardwoods. They lived in a beautiful cleared area on the coast, at the jungle's edge. Their bungalows were very airy, made of wood with coconut thatch roofs, and surrounded by orchids, frangipani, bougainvillea, hibiscus and jacaranda.

On returning to the ship that night, it took me a little time to appreciate just how beautiful the surroundings were in which these people lived.

Certainly they were isolated, but this price seemed worth it. At Tawau, the jungle grew right down to the sea, producing swamps full of monkeys and bright birds. Coral reefs and atolls guarded the entrance to the Sulu Sea. Once again, I felt glad I had opted for the Navy. Just how lucky I was I found on reading a CIW (Commissions and Warrants) list, which was lying on the wardroom table. These lists were the means by which the promotions and new drafts of all officers were announced, and they were eagerly studied. One of my contemporaries had, I saw, been moved from an English dockyard to an aircraft repair factory. Not for him the sun, the palm trees, golden sand, sharks all around and flying fish skimming away from the bows.

The Indonesians having caused no further trouble, we left Tawau for Hong Kong. Before leaving, however, we had one further unique experience: a game of rugby in a clearing in the jungle of Borneo. The opposition was raised from another forestry estate, this time the Borneo-Abaco Timber Company, producers of hemp and rubber. The match took place fifteen miles from Tawau, on a track which reminded me of the road to Achmelvich in north-west Sutherland. Hemp, I found, is a bush about twelve feet high. Rubber, in the form of latex, is drained directly from the tree into aluminium containers. On this estate, I met the doctor to the BA Timber Company who was accompanied by his wife. He was from Glasgow, she from Monifieth, near Dundee. Again, neither seemed to mind their isolation.

We left for Hong Kong after a very pleasant stay in a place seldom visited by one of HM ships. Yet again, however, our anticipation of a splendid time in Hong Kong was to be thwarted by the powers-that-be in London. And again, it was the fault of the Indonesians. This time they were threatening British, Dutch and American nationals on the island of Celebes, one of the four Greater Sunda Islands of Indonesia. Indonesia itself used to be called the Dutch East Indies. We were diverted to Manado in the north arm of the island of Celebes, where we were to be ready to evacuate eighty people of all three nationalities

Now we were getting even deeper into unknown parts of the Pacific. I knew that a battle had been fought in World War II between the Americans and Dutch on one side, and the Japanese on the other. This took place in the strait between Borneo and Celebes and resulted in a defeat for the Americans, with the Japanese gaining a foothold in Borneo and its important natural resources. The strait was called the Makassar Strait. All I knew of Makassar was that it was a town at the south end of Celebes which, in days gone by, had exported Makassar oil. This was a form of Victorian hair oil, hence the 'anti-makassars' which old ladies used to put on their best armchairs for protection.

At the last minute, the authorities realised that Manado harbour had not been properly cleared of mines left over from World War II. We were therefore to stay outside the harbour in deeper water and transport any people requiring evacuation in shallow draught boats. In the end, no one was evacuated. It was learned that the political temperature ashore was cooling and that the sight of a British warship close inshore might simply exacerbate the situation. From our point of view, this was not a problem, and we spent a great twenty-four hours cruising offshore along the coast of Celebes which, once again, was stunningly beautiful. When London eventually decided that all was well, we were, for the third time, given the order to sail for Hong Kong. The passage was to be via the poorly charted Celebes Sea, which is almost 3000 fathoms deep (18,000 ft) in places. Just to the north was the Mindanao Deep, the deepest water in the world. This lies just to the east of the Philippines, with a colossal depth of 37,000 ft. We then travelled through the Sulu Archipelago, along the coast of the southernmost Philippines, through the Balabac Strait and back into the South China Sea. Then north to Hong Kong or, as the Navy calls it, 'Honkers'.

We passed only two ships in the week it took us to get to Hong Kong, with the temperature dropping all the time. The days of films on the quarter-deck in the open air came to an end, as did the display of flying fish shooting out from beneath the bows. Occasionally a fish would land on the deck, and made very good eating. I had got used to the heat. On one day, which seemed quite cool, I found the temperature was still eighty-nine degrees. The maximum in Hong Kong just then was sixty-nine degrees and we wore blue uniform.

So what had this long diversion achieved? Maybe little beyond possible deterrence, but it had been a very enjoyable experience for me nonetheless.

7

Hong Kong

One of the problems of being a doctor on a small ship is the lack of work. At the same time, we were travelling in new and interesting places and I was keen to see as much as possible. With everyone else so busy, I did not wish to advertise my inactivity too obviously and therefore had to find a quiet place for spectating, or 'goofing' as it is known on aircraft carriers. This is not easy on a frigate but I did discover a place near a X gun platform, and I used this spot on many occasions, except when 'stand easy' was called on the ship's broadcast. Then, I would go right aft and observe the world from the depth charge rails.

A sea approach is the ideal way to view Hong Kong for the first time. *Crane* arrived in the early morning, just as cloud was rising from the Peak. The view of this remarkable place from the sea was stunning. Borneo, the mountains of Celebes, and even the tranquil setting of *Terror* at Singapore, paled into in comparison to the sight before us.

Hong Kong had a romantic history. In its early days, it had been the home of pirates. It had been ceded by China to Britain in two stages, after Britain had won the Opium Wars. The first followed the First Opium War, the second after the Second. At first, only Hong Kong Island was acquired, but the British felt that this did provide them with adequate control over this splendid harbour, which forms the channel that runs between the two parts of the colony. Accordingly, the Second Opium War was craftily initiated by Britain and, after it had been won, the mainland area was also acquired. This time it was ceded to Britain's new Crown Colony for ninety-nine years. Strangely, the cause of the Opium Wars, especially the Second, was Britain's anger at having its opium imports to China stopped. As a result of the widespread addiction the British supply of the drug was causing and the growing social consequences, the Chinese had decided enough was enough. The Japanese occupied Hong Kong for a few years during World War II, succeeding in reducing the population by more than half. Food shortages led many people to flee to mainland China.

Hong Kong's fine natural harbour, which extends between the island – of which Victoria is the 'capital', and the mainland area, Kowloon – had proved an ideal place for British merchants to anchor their opium carrying vessels. Now, on our arrival, the harbour was a mass of shipping activity, with both large and small vessels from many parts of the world. This, and the dramatic skyscrapers built on even the steepest parts of Victoria, helped to create our breath-taking first impression of Hong Kong. One skyscraper was built on ground so steep that there was a horizontal walk-way from the hillside to the top of the building. The smell of the harbour hung over all, unique but not offensive as in many other harbours. Even at this early hour, many ferries were running across the harbour. Numerous local boats were also on the move and these ranged from large, dignified junks to small sampans, both in great numbers. Sampans, which are about 15ft long, may be the only home that some Chinese ever know. They are only partially decked, if at all, and yet people sleep and cook on them, spreading an awning to keep out of the rain or the sun. Every kind of merchant ship was in harbour, as were warships, including aircraft carriers from Britain, Holland and America. Docks and jetties seemed to fill every bit of space on both sides of the harbour. Typhoon shelters were built to protect sampans and other small craft.

When we docked, I moved into HMS Tamar, the 'stone frigate' which was the Navy's headquarters in Hong Kong. Sick bay routine ashore was much the same as on a ship, but with more staff and room. Tamar was very different from Terror, being urban and noisy. Just opposite, was an area of open ground where the Japanese carried out executions during the war. The holiday atmosphere on ship was missing and was replaced by formality, this even extending to the presentation of the food, with the use of much mess silverware, including finger bowls. The food was very good and I discovered a brief passion for boiled eggs at breakfast.

The winter here had just finished and the monsoon season was beginning. In fact, a monsoon warning flag was flying at the harbour when we arrived. This heralded high winds, torrential rain and an electrical storm. I discovered that I had been allocated three nights of medical guard duty, which meant covering all ships and also all naval families on both sides of the harbour. The crossing was like negotiating a busy road during rush hour. Junks and sampans floated about and did not show lights at night, which added to the chaos. On

One of hundreds of junks in Hong Kong

my first duty period little was required. One trip across to Kowloon, this time on the Star Ferry instead of a naval launch, was to see a small girl with otitis media, an ear infection. Later I was to travel all over Hong Kong on both sides of the water. The naval base had been cast into gloom just before our arrival by the death of a young man in custody. He had been drinking, was brought in by the Naval Patrol and finished up in the cells. Unfortunately he had also fractured his skull which led to his death from intracranial bleeding. This is one of the scenarios dreaded by all casualty officers in all hospitals, and also by the police. It happens occasionally, however.

The ships were involved in refits of different kinds, so I now had time to explore this unique place – from the cloud-hidden houses on the Peak, to the long finger of the new runway at Kai Tak airport, sticking out into the harbour. Slightly further afield, were the small farms of the New Territories beyond Kowloon. These small farms provide a large part of the food supply of Hong Kong. Red China is thirty miles away from the sea, and we went on the Kowloon-Canton railway through the New Territories and as far as Westerners are permitted to travel. The furthest extent is at Sheung Shui near the border, the latter marked by a big arch with visible Chinese guards. On the way, the modern diesel train passed through the villages of Yaumati, Sha Tin, Taipo and Fanling. The overall impression was of rice paddies, oxen, children, flies and bicycles, with beggars on station platforms rattling their cans. It was said that a child born with a deformed limb, which meant they would not be able to work, had their deformity worsened by their parents to enable them to exist by begging. The smell of joss was everywhere.

Back on Hong Kong Island, I discovered just how difficult it was for the postal authorities to find me. I had been sent a letter from home, correctly addressed and stamped, but its progress had been circuitous. First it went to Singapore, then to *Mounts Bay*, then on to Hong Kong, then to *Opossum* which was in Plymouth, then to GPO London, then to Admiralty, then to Hong Kong again, then to *Cardigan Bay*, another ship of the 3rd Frigate Squadron, where it was seen by the squadron 'schoolie' and picked up by him for me.

I had to go up twice by cable car to the small Naval Hospital on the Peak. Two men from *Modeste* had been admitted there with suspected active tuberculosis, which meant more chest X-rays for the two hundred others.

From the hospital there was a tremendous view of the island when the cloud lifted. It was usual for the cloud not to clear at all for days at a time, and the people in the hospital would ask, 'What's the weather like down below?'

The town of Victoria was a mixture of the sophisticated and the ordinary, Women all seemed to be slim, and many wore the close-fitting *cheongsam*, a dress which would not be suitable for Europeans. Babies were carried in bright silk squares on their mother's back, sometimes having the head supported by a separate bandage. Sometimes other children in the family carried their little brothers or sisters in this way. A characteristic sound in the streets is the clack of Maj Jong pieces coming from open doorways, as pedestrians pass by. This game is popular with older men.

At the Lok Yu hall of Hong Kong University we saw a performance of *As You Like It*, given in English by a Chinese cast. This was presented by a student company called 'The Masquers' of whom the president was none other than Edmund Blunden. Blunden was the professor of English at Hong Kong University and was well known in Britain for his poetry and literary criticism. He at least had a hand in this Shakespeare production and himself took the part of Adam, the old servant of Oliver. There were Chinese sub-titles and an expensive-looking programme supported by various traders. 'All the women's costumes' said one half-page advertisement, 'were tailored by Oi Lai, lb Breezy Terrace, Bonham Road, Hong Kong.' The programme also contained a page of literary quotations, amongst which was one from something called 'Old China' of 1823. 'We squeezed out our shillings apiece,' it said, 'to sit three or four times in a season in the one shilling gallery … and when the curtain drew up, what cared we for our place in the house, or what mattered it where we were sitting, when our thoughts were with Rosalind in Arden, or with Viola at the Court of Illyria?' All in all, a most enjoyable evening.

Kowloon is the main shopping area, with shops in modem arcades, much haggling and many fake goods. We saw real jade, silks and ivory, as well as cedar wood furniture. A man tried to sell us a 'lamp post' when he meant a table lamp. Trams clattered by with first-class upstairs and third-class below. The streets had fleets of new Mercedes and Vauxhall taxis, as well as many rickshaws. There was much spitting, which may have been related to the two and a half thousand new cases of tuberculosis notified in the city during the past year. Women in coolie hats worked alongside men on building sites, sometimes after midnight.

Hong Kong is certainly different from the West. We saw two policemen, for example, running after an escaped prisoner. The man casually jumped over a woman who was screaming as she squatted on the pavement. She was obviously in labour and was surrounded by an interested but unhelpful crowd.

The good news was that the Japanese cruise was still on and I was going on *Modeste*. I thought that we had missed the chance because of the Borneo episode, but happily this assumption proved incorrect. I therefore moved back on to *Modeste*, but, before we left, the ship took part in Exercise Festoon. This was an anti-submarine exercise carried out with Australian and New Zealand ships. We travelled south to carry out the exercise, which meant an improvement in the weather and a rise in temperature. The cabin reached eighty-nine degrees and when the fan broke I spent the rest of the night on a camp bed under the stars, with a calm sea.

As we were going to Japan on a 'showing the flag' cruise and escorting the C in C in his despatch vessel, it was necessary for *Modeste* to look her best. Therefore, when we returned from Festoon, the ship's 'side party' painted the side. This is part of the work done by enthusiastic Chinese women. The story of these women is an interesting one and is related as follows.

Every British warship coming to Hong Kong has its own sampan, this being crewed by four or five Chinese women. These are self-appointed 'side parties', whose main job is to paint the side of the ship. This they do with aplomb, and they are therefore popular with the ship's company, whose work they do for them. Not only do they paint the ship's side, but they will also do any other work, sometimes continuing long after the sailors have finished for the day. Amazingly, they don't accept money from the ship as payment. All they want is leftovers after the crew's meals, old ropes and boxes, and even empty food tins which they flatten. The sailors keep empty baked bean tins for them, which they then sell to the peasant farmers in the New Territories for good prices. When we were at Sheung Shui, for example, an old man tried to sell us an empty Carnation Milk tin. At the end of each day's work the women can be seen loading their spoils onto their sampan. They cheerfully put up with leg pulling, but if this gets too serious they quickly stop it with a remark such as, 'You no skylark, huh,' accompanied by a look sufficient to drop the unfortunate man in his tracks. The *Crane's* side party had a banner on their sampan, made from a white sheet. In red paint it proclaimed 'HMS *Crane's* Side Party'. These side parties guard their self-proclaimed rights jealously, but, on one occasion, we saw a rival sampan attempting to drag a fishing net under the ship in a search for tins and bottles. They were quickly scared away by the first lieutenant with appropriately salty language. It is a tradition that when a ship sets off and leaves for the UK their side party sees them off with Chinese fire-crackers fired from their sampan. These they fire all at once, making a distinctive noise heard all over the harbour. We were now all set for the much-anticipated Japanese cruise.

8

Japan and Korea

We left at five in the morning on our cruise. It was taking place at the best time of year: the season when the cherry blossom flowered along the streets of Japan. In fact, the weather was so poor on the journey north, that it felt like the darkest of winters.

On this cruise, *Modeste* accompanied the Navy's Far East Station commander-in-chief on his despatch vessel *Alert*. These were both small ships. *Modeste* is a modified Black Swan class frigate, displacing 1,500 tons and under 300 ft long. Its complement was 200 and its armament has already been detailed. One could only stand upright at a few places below the upper deck. The whole thing was a maze of pipes, cables, fans, ventilation shafts, fuse boxes, alarm bells, buzzers, internal broadcast loudspeakers, generators, shell hoists and, running round all of this, a fire main with large valves controlled by big wheels. There was an incessant smell of cooking and fuel oil and constant noise from the engine room. Generators ran non-stop, both in harbour as well as at sea, which at first made sleeping difficult. Officers' quarters, accessed by two near-vertical ladders, were right aft, except for a crowded depth charge store. Living conditions for the ship's company up forward were much the same, only more crowded. Hammocks are considered comfortable, especially in rough weather.

Modeste *and C-in-C's despatch vessel* Alert *at Tokyo, dressed overall*

It is not surprising, therefore, that with the continual noise and the violent motion of this small ship in bad weather, some people suffered from sea sickness. In fact, a few unfortunates suffered from this miserable condition whenever these ships put to sea, whatever the weather. Happily I was immune, but *Modeste's* new electrical officer spent most of the passage to Japan confined to his bunk. Our four supernumerary Chinese were even worse off. They actually lived and worked in the depth charge store, right in the stern. These tiny men, poor sailors during the best of times, were to give me some anxiety on the journey to Japan. They were additional to the ship's company, employed as unpaid tradesmen known as *dhobi*, who existed on what they charged the ship's company for washing and ironing clothes, and for shoe-making and repair. The cobbler sat on a box in a space about 3 sq. ft located behind a door, with his work on his knee. The evil looking depth charges which surrounded them did not seem to worry them at all.

At this stage I wrote a letter home:

> As I write, we are passing the outlying islets of the south island of Japan, Kyushu. The passage up from Hong Kong has been in a very rough sea with

*quite a bit of damage to the ship, which is small, and much sea sickness. The
new Electrical Officer has spent most of the time in his bunk and I've had to
turn in our Chinese 'No.3 Dhobi' in the sickbay. After prolonged vomiting he
lost consciousness twice, and had a minor fit. He had not eaten for five days.
We lost time because of the weather, and are now pressing on at full speed
through seas which are still big enough to send sheets of spray over the bridge
when the bows dip under. Nowhere on the upper deck is safe from breaking
waves, and all hatches have to be firmly shut. By good chance I have a scuttle,
porthole to you, at the head of my bunk which gives me a view of the world
from ten feet above the sea when I lie down. This is normally good fun, and
is even more so at present when full daylight is diffused by green water every
time we roll to starboard. There is a pendulum-type angle-of-roll measuring
device in the wardroom but I can judge the degree of roll simply by seeing how
long my view is a watery one. The temperature is falling as we go north.
We've just passed Okinawa after leaving the Formosa Strait and fans are now
off. Must see if my steward, Chen Yow, can find a blanket. His English is
limited to 'Good morning' and 'Soos, sir?' which means 'Do you want your
shoes cleaned today?' Have just finished Linklater's 'A Year of Space' It gives
a good description of this part of the world, and also of life on Cardigan Bay
of this squadron, which took him to post-war Korea. There has just been
a yell and a crash from outside my cabin as someone dropped this evening's
dinner after the ship gave a heavy lurch. I hear we have eight feet of water
in the cable locker and that the forepeak is flooded. We are still, however, at
full speed, as we must arrive at Yokosuka on Monday at 1am. This letter will
be posted from there.*

Just after we left Hong Kong there occurred a minor disagreement, the
kind of event which was predicted in the Divisional Course at Portsmouth.
The *Far East Station Guide Book* said that all ships visiting Korea had to have
everyone immunised against typhus. The Naval Medical Officer of Health
(MOH) called me to his office to remind me of this necessity. Accordingly,
I laid on a stock of this vaccine and, after we sailed, went to see the captain.
'Can't be done. Doc!' he said, 'we're mounting a guard of honour when we
arrive in Tokyo and I can't have the sailors with sore arms.' I told him about

the orders from the MOH and the *Guide Book*. He remained adamant and, thus, a problem arose. I understood his position, but an outbreak of typhus would be pretty serious, not to mention the clear instructions I had received to carry out this task. I remembered the chief petty officer in Portsmouth saying, 'If you find yourself in direct disagreement with an order from the executive you must get it in writing.' I really did not wish to go down this road but, on thinking it over, decided I had no alternative. Accordingly, I went to see the captain again and, taking a deep breath, explained the situation a second time and asked for his order in writing. 'Certainly, Doc', he said, 'type it out and I will sign it.' So I did so and he signed it, quite pleased with himself and without thinking twice about it. I, however, was puzzled. This was similar to the 'appendicitis' issue during Exercise Fotex, when I was not allowed to examine the man. Was this the Navy's way of doing things? In the end nobody got typhus and we did mount our guard of honour. From the captain's attitude thereafter, it seemed as if he hadn't even registered the whole episode. So everything had passed off successfully, for which I was glad.

The voyage progressed at speed and damage just had to be accepted. We arrived in Japan at Yokosuka, on the island of Honshu. This quickly proved a disappointing, Americanised place, with absolutely nobody and nothing in sight. Certainly a poor way to arrive in a new country, but we knew that the next port of call was to be the big one.

A dramatic sight awaited us as we moved up along the coast towards Tokyo. On the way, we had a good view of the snow-capped Fujiyama, with the clearly visible conical peak just below cloud level. This was lucky for us, as it is not always in view. The liner *Caronia* was sitting nearby with her bows on a rock, having, we believed, just knocked over a lighthouse. She had lain near us in Hong Kong, crammed with American tourists.

A buzz began to grow about the ship as we drew closer to Japan's capital. This was a 'showing the flag' trip pure and simple, with the C in C along for good measure. Everything, therefore, had to look its best. There was bound to be a bit of 'social tittery', as the Navy calls it, and we had been warned that the occupants of the wardroom would be involved. This was to be a change from my time spent with the crypto team and from recording the fall of shot as the four-inch guns fired broadsides.

The approach to Tokyo harbour is lined with many miles of pearl beds. These look like the business ends of gigantic hairbrushes held just below the surface. Here, pearls are provided for Mikimoto's in Tokyo, a world-famous pearl dealer. As a result of being an official visit of the British C in C in the Far East to Japan's capital, our arrival in Tokyo was all pomp and ceremony. The two ships were 'dressed overall', which means they were displaying a continuous array of flags from the jackstaff in the bows, via the mast-head, to the ensign staff at the stern. The order in which the flags are displayed on naval ships is never haphazard but must conform to certain regulations. The two ships lay alongside one another against the wall in Tokyo's harbour and, with their fresh coat of grey paint, were a splendid sight. The presence in the harbour of a Japanese naval ship flying the 'Rising Sun' made us pause a little, but this was an occasion to be enjoyed.

During our stay there were gun salutes, official calls, receptions, and much wearing of 'tiddly', or very formal, uniforms. A reception on Alert, the C in C's despatch vessel, gave me a glimpse of a different world. This was a gathering of the great and the good and, as anticipated, we of Modeste were roped in to help the small number of Alert's officers to host the event. I met foreign military and naval attaches, and I talked with the Turkish military attaché about Ankara. I also conversed with the New Zealand ambassador's wife, the British consul, an American colonel who administered the UN occupation troops in Korea, and two members of the Japanese imperial household.. It was a colourful scene on Alert's awning-covered quarterdeck, with many strange uniforms and decorations. The Japanese women wore kimonos, and there was much bowing with hands clasped and hissing through the teeth. This hissing means something polite in Japanese. Royal Marines in their best uniforms handed around the small eats.

The reception was held on Alert's quarterdeck. As on Modeste's, this was a difficult place for comfortable footing, especially for women in light shoes, because of the presence of 'ring bolts'. These are let into the deck seemingly at random and stand proud of it by about three inches. They are painted the same colour as the deck and are therefore difficult to see. Such was this the case that one of Modeste's sailors had appropriate tattoos on each of his shins. These each showed an eye, with 'Port ring bolt lookout' beneath one and

'Starboard ring bolt lookout' beneath the other. Light shoes do not go well with warships.

From my point of view, however, my visit to Tokyo was made worthwhile by a cocktail party at the British Embassy. There, I met an English girl who could only be described as stunning. The result was that I saw less of Tokyo and more of its fabulous night life than I expected. The embassy girl, who shared a house with another girl also from the embassy, managed to wangle the use of the ambassadorial Rolls, with its flag concealed in a leather sheath. This meant less exposure to Tokyo's taxis, or 'Kamikazi cars' as they were known after the Japanese suicide pilots of World War II. It seems that these are paid by the number of fares they receive, rather than the distance they travel, which means they move at great speed. Every day there are accidents involving these cars.

The main street in Tokyo is the Ginza, which is bigger and better than Regent Street, and just as expensive. I took the embassy girl to Suahiro's on this street. Suahiro's is one of the city's quality restaurants, very different from restaurants at home. Shoes are left at the door and one sits cross-legged on cushions on the floor, with the table being about eighteen inches high. The floor is covered in matting and the walls of the individual 'eating rooms' consist of lightweight sliding panels about 8ft high. The wooden framework of these panels is made of little squares or panes, filled in with a light parchment. Men are served first. We ate sukiyaki, a dish of sliced meat simmered with vegetables and served in a delicious sauce, and drank sake, an alcoholic drink made from rice.

As predicted, the streets were lined with cherry trees in bloom. Many Japanese wore facemasks, probably to protect against some flu-type illness in the city at that time. It has to be admitted that many of the men seemed extremely ugly by European standards, especially the dockyard workers. They were short-necked and squat with thick black hair, cut to leave rigid ends sticking out from under their khaki workmen's caps. Slant-eyed and inscrutable, they seldom smiled. We passed an amusing figure walking down the Ginza. He was dressed in a black kimono-type garment and in addition to a facemask, wore a cap at an angle and leather sandals. He carried a sandwich board which proclaimed in Japanese that he had given his life for so-many

Main street, Tokyo (The Ginza).

yen. Why he had given it, I did not find out. *The Bridge on the River Kwai* was showing in Tokyo. Some of our sailors went to see it and reported that the Japanese general was regarded as true to life and the plight of the British troops was greeted with laughter.

Before we left for Kobe, three hundred and sixty miles to the south, I had just time to see the Emperor's Palace, the royal and spiritual centre of the country. This sits in vast grounds surrounded by ornate walls and a broad moat. The Diet, Japan's parliament, is built of an unusual light-brown stone.

Kobe is said to resemble Swansea, meaning that it is not a very beautiful place. From our somewhat uncivilised point of view, two things were outstanding. The first was a restaurant to which a few of us went to eat the house specialty, Kobe beef. This is world famous and the beef used is Aberdeen Angus. It certainly lived up to its reputation. The second was a wonderful shopping area called the Motomashi. This was an open arcade, lined with cherry blossom. There were shops of all kinds, from those selling furniture to those telling fortunes. We spent a lot of time in toy shops winding up all kinds of mechanical toy. Most cabins later sported walking spacemen, arm-waving gorillas, flirty ladybirds and talking dolls. This time the receptions were at the Kobe Club, a European establishment, and again on *Alert.*. Strangely only two Japanese were present at the latter, and we from *Modeste's* wardroom were once more called upon to help as hosts.

After Kobe, we had a fascinating passage through the Inland Sea, between the islands of Honshu and Shikoku. This reminded me of northwest Scotland, except that it was greener. Barren mountains fringed the narrow sea on each side as we passed through on a cold, misty day of drizzling rain. At times, the channel was only a few hundred yards wide, and we had a good view of fishing villages, which resembled those on the Aberdeenshire coast, although their boats were quite different. They are powered by sail and sit high in the water. Emerging from the Inland Sea and on to the Korea Strait, we ran into thick fog, where the visibility was reduced to fifty yards. Radar was much appreciated as we went through the narrows and rendezvoused with *St Brides*, who joined us for the rest of the cruise. She had travelled straight up from Singapore, with one day spent in Hong Kong. My work, when we were in harbour, doubled to half an hour per day.

We called at Sasebo, very close to Nagasaki on the island of Kyushu, for one day only. This is a coal mining area and, when we were there, it seemed overrun by American troops. For some reason, the powers-that-be had decreed that we were to return here on the way back to Yokosuka.

Although we were on a 'showing the flag' cruise, daily life on the ship continued more or less unchanged. I wrote another letter home, in which I took the opportunity to explain the mysteries of 'tots' and 'grog', or 'Nelson's blood' as rum is known.

Well, the pipe 'Leading hands of messes muster for rum' has just been made on the ship's broadcast, which means it's noon. Leading hands of the various messes now go to the cox'n's shack where each gets a carefully measured amount of rum to provide a 'tot' for each man in his mess. The container is then carefully carried back to the mess and the leading hand distributes it. Younger men do not get a 'tot' but do get 'grog', which is rum diluted with water. 'Tot time' precedes the lunch break from the work of the ship, a break ended by the old pipe, 'Out pipes.' Much lore is associated with rum dispensing, the oldest trick, which everyone knows, is when the 'dispenser' leaves his thumb in the rum each time he gives someone a tot. This means he has so many 'thumb's worth' left over at the end, which, of course, he keeps for himself. For me, noon means it's time I had some lunch. After all, I did do fifteen minutes work this morning.

Twenty-four hours after leaving Sasebo, we were passing through the Yellow Sea, bound for South Korea. The Yellow Sea is well named, being dirty orange-yellow in colour from the mud brought down from China's Yellow River. Because of the mud, we had to come to anchor off Inchon, the port for South Korea's capital, Seoul. Both these places were largely ruined by the war. The countryside was devastated and the people looked very poor. We realised that this was the effect of war, but that did not stop us going to a lavish reception for the C in C, given by the senior American general in charge of UN occupying forces.

This was the first time that any of us had gone to a cocktail party by land, sea and air. As we were required to anchor two miles off-shore, the first part of the journey was made in the ship's motor boat. The thirty miles from Inchon to Seoul was by US army helicopter and the last leg was made in large American cars. From the helicopter, we had views of barren red hills and mile after mile of paddy fields. After the official entertainment, we discovered that the British military also had a presence in South Korea and three of us gate-crashed a small party given by an officer in the Lancers. He was not best pleased to see us but recovered manfully, saying 'OK then. One drink and you go. Right?' We did, but not before I insisted on getting a drink for a pretty American girl, who had asked what the red stripe between the two gold ones on my sleeve meant. 'Whee-ee!' she said when I told her. She asked for a 'Creme de menthe and vodka frappe, please,' which I thought rather silly. The Lancer, however, came up trumps. We returned to the ship that evening by illegal means, on a road which, at times, disappeared, leaving only uneven sand dunes.

Next day we toured Seoul. This included a visit to the house of President Synghman Rhee, with guards behind every tree. In the former Royal palace – Korea was a monarchy until fifty years ago – there was a board bearing the following inscription:

Seen in Seoul, South Korea

SUN JUNG CHUN
BUILT IN 1653, THE FOURTH YEAR OF HYUKONG'S REIGN
(17ᵀᴴ KING OF THE YI DYNASTY)
THIS IS THE ONLY BLUE-TITLED PALACE IN KOREA, PROBABLY
THE ONLY ONE OF ITS KIND IN THE FAR EAST. USED FOR SECRET
CONFERENCES WITH TOP-RANKING MINISTERS, MANY POLITICAL
INTRIGUES ORIGINATED FROM THIS PALACE. IT WAS ALSO USED
FOR GIVING AUDIENCES TO FOREIGN DIPLOMATS.

The ordinary people of South Korea, even in the capital, still looked poor and shattered. Many bridges were still down, so we returned from Seoul on a 'non-road' with many detours. A curfew was in force and everything was being controlled by American military police in white steel helmets and jeeps. Three days was long enough to spend in this grim place, but there were two happenings which relieved the misery.

Before we left Inchon, our captain asked the wardroom to provide someone to help entertain guests in his cabin. This duty was shared among us by rota and it was now my turn. The captain managed to get the ship's cooks to provide the best dinner I had eaten for months. He had invited the First Secretary of the British Embassy in Seoul, but more importantly, he had managed to find some smooth and glamorous women. With alcohol in free-flow, the evening was undoubtedly a success.

The other event of note was the arrival on board of Swiss and Swedish officers of the Neutral Nations Supervisory Commission. Among them was the doctor who went with the successful Swiss Everest expedition. They got four men to the top of Everest, and he himself reached the South Col. He was a very nice chap, who insisted on seeing our sick bay and then touring the ship. He was so interested in everything that was going on, that I eventually had to tell him that we were sailing in half an hour, and that his boat was alongside. He was not altogether happy about how the medical aspects of his expedition had been recounted in the official book, *The Everest-Lhotse Adventure*.

Peng Yong Do is an island twelve miles off the coast of North Korea, just north of the 38th parallel. Also known as 'PYD', the Americans had a radar base there, from which they observed the Communists. There were only a handful of American officers, all carrying pistols in hip holsters, as there were six thousand Communist refugees on the island. The presence of the latter meant that our sailors were not allowed ashore, especially as it was the Communist May Day. Three officers were, however, invited to have lunch and, after considerable elbowing, and playing the 'find out what medical facilities are available' card, I was one of the lucky ones. The Americans have a single living hut like an Antarctic base and receive a supply plane every two weeks. The only buildings on the island were mud and thatch dwellings used by the Koreans. The Americans fed us well and were delighted to see us, four of them

Transferring to St Bride's Bay

coming out to the ship before we left. Their tour on the island lasted for one year.

It was now time to return to Japan. On the way back to Sasebo, *St Brides* wanted to practise their jackstay transfer drill. Being the only squadron officer available, I was required to go across. The cheeky suggestion by me that I was the squadron MO and not the squadron test-weight, was treated by all with great amusement. I went over at 11am and checked their sick list, examined their captain for a life insurance policy, and had lunch. Then, after a good visit, I went back to *Modeste* by the same method.

Our stay in Sasebo was mercifully short and then we continued on to Beppu, a hot-spring site, and completely free from Americans. This Japanese holiday resort was a mass of cherry blossom. We played rugby against 'All Beppu' with no goalposts at one end. Place kicks were taken from corresponding points on each side. A cocktail party was held on *Modeste* to which local Japanese dignitaries were invited. The mayor gave a speech of thanks which, of course, we did not understand. We did understand, albeit with a faint shudder, his exhortation to his fellow guests to toast us by shouting 'Banzai'. This was also the 'over the top' cry used by Japanese troops.

From Beppu we travelled to Nagoya, an industrial town which lay four miles from the jetty. The ship was once again open to visitors and we were amazed that we received three thousand in one afternoon. There was a nice little event as we left for our last port of call – a return visit to Yokosuka. A long breakwater stretches out into Nagoya Bay. On the end of the breakwater, there is a low lighthouse. As we passed, they dipped the Japanese flag and played a cracked record of 'Auld Lang Syne'. On the way back to Yokosuka, the SBA on *St Brides Bay* thought he had developed diphtheria, which for me meant another two trips by jackstay. I was happy that he had not, and was quite proud of my further ship-to-ship travel. In fact the navigator of *Crane* and I shared the record for the number of transfers made in this way during this commission.

Just before arriving at Yokosuka we carried out an anti-submarine exercise with an American submarine. Our Japanese cruise finished with a return visit to Yokosuka, which was still the dullest of places. I compensated for this with two trips to Tokyo, on the fast train via Yokohama.

9

Back to Hong Kong

We left Japan just as the Third Asian Games were beginning in Tokyo. We had called at more places than is usual for a British warship 'showing the flag' here. Many people came to take a look over the ship, among them five medical students from Nagoya who were going into their navy on graduation. We had, by now, seen two of their smaller warships and noticed with mixed feelings that they were still flying the 'Rising Sun' at the stern. But these medical students were nice lads. They were visibly impressed by our cramped sick bay and its two gimballed bunks. They were also fascinated by the way in which everything in the sick bay was secured against the ship's often violent movement at sea. Some of their surgical terms are in English and the same as ours, and they had even brought their notebooks to show me.

Mount Fujiyama was a splendid sight with its even snow cone. Impressive also, though in a different sense, was the rumbling sound of the shelling of Quemoy, a Chinese dispute, the history of which I did not know. Travelling south, the weather was fine all the way except on the first day, when a particularly heavy roll toppled a fish tank. This was sad for the man who bought it, but good news for the militant anti-tropical fish league.

There was a tragedy on *Crane* when she was returning from another visit to Japan shortly after us, and travelling slightly further south. The gunnery

Leaving Tokyo for Hong Kong. Mount Fujiyama is on the horizon

officer, who had been the first officer I had met, after the captain, when I first joined the ship, developed respiratory poliomyelitis. The chances of recovery from this illness are very slight and, on a ship at sea miles from land, probably nil. There was no doctor on board. They altered course for Okinawa, the nearest land, but he died on the way. The captain wrote the following tribute to him, which appeared in the ship's end-of-commission magazine. It was accompanied by a photograph and edged in black.

It was a very sad moment indeed when I had to inform the ship's company that Lieutenant Anderson had died during the night of poliomyelitis. Lieutenant Anderson was the senior lieutenant, ship's gunnery officer and sports officer. His death left an empty place in the hearts of all of us, and it is difficult to say whether we will remember him more for his efficiency, determination and good humour, or for his enthusiasm in the field of play, swimming pool and squash court. He possessed all these qualities in the fullest measure and combined them with sound judgement and the utmost integrity.

He was buried at sea with full Naval Honours, five hundred miles east of Formosa.

The ship's company has presented a squadron trophy for football, to be known as the Anderson Cup. This cup will serve as a memorial for all of us who served with Lieutenant Anderson in *Crane,* and for the many others within the Third Frigate Squadron who knew him for the excellent officer and good-natured shipmate that he was.

On return to Hong Kong the ship was held in quarantine at a buoy, until the risk of infection to others was past. This was a sad ending to their trip.

The highlight of our own journey south was undoubtedly a 'NEX', or 'Night Encounter Exercise'. We were told that another RN ship was heading north through the Formosa Strait on a reciprocal course to ours. The timing was approximate, but we were to pass in the hours of darkness, and to imagine that the other ship was hostile. The ship that 'survived' this encounter was to be the one that fired first, illuminating the other with one round of four-inch star shell. There was quite a bit of merchant shipping around, including unlit junks, so care was needed in selecting who to illuminate. The captain placed extra lookouts, and the radar, which was not very good, was watched carefully. One round of star shell was loaded in 'A' turret. Everyone then settled down to wait on this calm, almost moonless night.

Suddenly, dark red flames were spotted on our starboard bow. Fire at sea is a major emergency and the captain decided to abandon the exercise at once. We set off at speed to help the burning ship. Two minutes later a star shell exploded directly above us. We remained embarrassingly lit up by the brilliant light, as it descended slowly to the sea on its parachute, and the 'burning ship' altered course and approached us rapidly. Just as the intense white light went out when it hit the sea, the lines of a destroyer became visible. We had to endure laughter on their loud-hailer as they extinguished the burning oil drum, which they had secured to their forecastle. They closed with us and, as they swept past in the weak moonlight, triumphant cries of 'Oggy, oggy, oggy!' came over the water from the men on the deck of this Plymouth-based ship. She had only recently arrived from the UK so all our defeated sailors could think of to shout back was, 'Get some sea time in!'

On our approach to Hong Kong from Japan, two hundred and seventy junks were visible at the same time, all fishing. They were a problem at night as they seldom carry lights. Our response, when one was particularly troublesome, was to hold him in the Aldis beam for a few minutes.

At this time, the Royal Navy ships in Hong Kong were the cruisers *Newcastle* and *Newfoundland* plus New Zealand's *Royalist*, the destroyers *Cheviot* and *Cavalier* with HMS *Voyager*, the carrier *Bulwark*, and various inshore mine sweeper and motor launch flotillas.

Coming back to Hong Kong felt like coming home after the holidays. I lived for a time in the relative comfort of *Tamar* and, as the frigates were across the harbour in Kowloon, it was a bit like going to the office every morning. I either went over in a naval launch, or used one of the small civilian ferries. One morning Hong Kong was subjected to the peripheral effects of a typhoon near the Philippines. The high wind and rain, which in the tropics can fall in walls, meant that it took a long time to cross the harbour. I had to go right into town to get one of the big ferries. Contingency plans were in place should the colony be hit by the full force of the typhoon. Some ships

Naval shipping in Hong Kong

Aircraft carrier Bulwark *and Dutch launch*

had stopped shore leave, the cruisers were to go to sea, and the destroyers and frigates to buoys.

Entertainment, however, went ahead as usual. The orchestra of the Korean Broadcasting System gave a concert, which was poor. Sunday evening cinema was held in the Hong Kong Yacht Club in the open air, surrounded by sampans in the typhoon shelter. Social life was indeed our main focus at this time. *Modeste* gave its farewell party before leaving for Singapore and home. RNH Hong Kong threw a dinner and, as most ships of the Far East fleet were in harbour, a good number of the 'red braid shower' turned up. Another night, six of us went on a euphemistically named 'clinical run ashore'. This meant a round of some of the hundreds of nightclubs in the town, which finished abruptly at 3.30am, when the Arizona nightclub was raided by the police. We made a rapid exit via a side door, as the place was out of bounds.

Sixty cases of a flu-like illness occurred on *Modeste* in five days. There was no infection ashore and I sent specimens to the Virus Research Lab in Singapore. The capacity of the sick bay was increased by a hundred percent

Motor launches of Hong Kong flotilla

by means of slinging two hammocks. The criteria for admission to the sick bay were arbitrary. With so many ill it was difficult to select the worst. The rest had to just keep going and work the ship, as the captain would only put back the ship's programme by one day. I did manage to stop all participation in football and other active sports, considering them dangerous for people with a viraemia.

My home during this period was the captain's sea cabin, a cubby hole near the bridge. The name 'sea cabin' refers to the cabin he can occupy if his presence might be sought urgently by the officer of the watch. As we had been anchoring every night at different bays around Hong Kong Island, the captain had been able to sleep in his main cabin. In fact, I never saw a sea cabin used except by transient people like myself. Some of the bays around Hong Kong Island have romantic names such as Repulse Bay, Deep Water Bay, Junk Bay and Flying Fish Bay. There is also Sulphur Channel and Stonecutters' Island.

This leisurely progress around the island was interrupted when it was realised that the requisite depth charge firings had not been carried out. Accordingly, we set off one morning to find a sufficient depth of water to undertake the task. I found a good vantage point at the rear of the bridge and saw the charges being projected into the air from the mechanical throwers, mounted on the port and starboard quarters. At the same time, charges were rolled into the sea from the depth charge rails right aft. With the satisfying explosion, I saw the mast whip and a cloud of black smoke emerge from the funnel. But immediately after, the telephone on the bridge rang. It was the engine room, reporting that we had blown a hole in the side of the ship, which was admitting water. Faces were red as the course was reversed and we returned to harbour. Faces were even redder when it was found necessary to go into dry dock for repairs. The cause of this mishap I did not accurately discover. Either the charges had been set to go off before they were deep enough, or the water was not sufficiently deep. It did, however, create a lovely loud bang.

HMSS *Dampier* arrived in Hong Kong to store ship and pick up her new doctor. HMSS stands for 'Her Majesty's Survey Ship', of which the Navy has three. *Dampier* looked very smart in her all-white paint. Her doctor, who had been living in *Tamar* since flying out from the UK, showed me around her. The ship was air-conditioned and his cabin was roomy and well fitted out. It would need to be, as they were to spend up to two months at a stretch sitting off the east coast of Malaya, surveying the sea bed and charting the coastline. It was surprising to learn that huge areas of the sea had not been charted at all. In some areas, such as the western tip of New Guinea, the few soundings were made by lead lines and sailing ships. The names of these ships are recorded on even modern charts, alongside their findings and the date of sounding. *Dampier's* doctor was to collect plankton, and the British Museum had asked him to collect spiders from their survey points ashore. I felt he had a good job, probably second only to mine.

I had heard of some other national service officers in the Far East. Of twenty-four, only three were doctors. These were, myself on the frigates, one on a cruiser and another in charge of the Asian hospital in Singapore. Of those who joined the Navy on the same day as I did, one was in Sheerness dockyard looking after 'dockyard mateys', one was a factory doctor in an aircraft repair section near Bath, two were at Naval air stations in the UK, one was in Plymouth, and one was at RNH Haslar, Portsmouth. One had not

St Brides Bay *at Hong Hong*

moved from RNH Chatham and only two had received what I considered good postings, namely frigates in the Med and the Persian Gulf. The Gulf man I met later and quickly revised my opinion, as he was seriously bored. The three surgeon lieutenants who worked full-time from Tamar were all married and accompanied by their wives and families. They never went to sea in the three years of their short service commissions and spent a good deal of time playing billiards. Later I heard of a contemporary of mine who had spent all his time at a grim dockyard in England.. He felt that, having opted for the Navy, he really ought to get some sea-time in, before his two years were up. He explained things to some senior person and was sent for three weeks as a relief doctor on HMS *Russell*. Unfortunately, she was on fishery protection duties, off the coast of Iceland, and it was winter. I thought myself very fortunate.

Just before leaving for Singapore and a stay in the luxury of *Terror*, I had three interesting invitations. The first was to a little wooden inshore mine sweeper. This ran around Hong Kong waters, especially the bays of the New Territories, looking for smugglers. She had only two officers, one of whom was a Scot. If I was able to arrange it, I was to go on a three-day patrol with them. The second was an invitation to see over an American submarine, the USS *Rasher*. She was credited with sinking twenty-two ships in World War II, a total of 99,901 tons. This was the second highest tonnage sunk by any US submarine and entitled her to fly a special Presidential pennant.

The third was an invitation to dinner on Stonecutters Island. The survey ship's doctor and I spent a pleasant evening with the man who ran the dockyard surgery. His wife had just been to Peking. It was good to eat in home surroundings with ample second helpings of home cooking. After dinner, we sat out on the terrace, looking at the breathtaking sight of Hong Kong by night, with the lights and neon signs going all the way up the Peak. We came back ashore on a dockyard MFV, a Scottish-built seine net boat.

10

The Persian Gulf

We had a quiet trip to Singapore on *St Brides Bay*, being out of sight of land most of the time. It felt good to meet *Modeste* again, or the 'Fighting Forty Two' as she was known. She was shortly to leave Singapore for home, and then decommissioning. I moved back into the comfort of *Terror*, expecting to stay in Singapore for at least two months. The prospect of more space, less noise, good food and attractive surroundings was appealing, but, alas, it was not to be. The ironic phrase 'Haven't you heard? It's all been changed!' may have originated in the Army, but the Navy could change its plans just as suddenly. It took only two days for the anticipation of hedonism to disappear.

On the second evening back, I went with two medics from *Terror*, and one from the destroyers, on a 'run ashore' in Singapore town. We started with a meal at Bugis Street or, more accurately, on Bugis Street, because one actually eats at tables on the street. This was out-of-bounds to Service personnel, but famous for its good Chinese food. One guy wanted to stay longer in this tough area and would not be persuaded to come back with us. We had no option but to leave him and heard later that he had been assaulted and robbed. The 'run ashore' included visits to the 'Halfway House' at Bukit Timah, the Tanglin Club, the Tanglin Inn, and the 'New World' for 'taxi dancing'. The 'New

World also had a fairground-type shooting gallery, which used compressed air cannons instead of the usual air rifles. At the end of the evening, those of us who were left hired a taxi for the trip back across the island. The immediate sequel I recounted in a letter:

> *It's 5.30 am. Three hours ago three of us came through the gates of Terror in a taxi from Singapore town. The two sentries on the gate, rifles slung over their shoulders, stopped the car*
>
> *'Is Surgeon Lieutenant Yule in this car?'*
>
> *'That's me.'*
>
> *'Sir, the duty Staff Commander is looking for you. Please get in touch with him.'*
>
> *'At three in the morning?'*
>
> *'Yes sir.'*
>
> *I phoned him. 'Oh yes, doe' he said. 'It seems that King Faisal of Iraq has been murdered in a coup. There may be trouble for the Brits there so we're backing up the two Gulf frigates from here. Modeste is going and we want you to go with her. Better pack your things.'*

I sat down on my bed with a lot to think about. Only yesterday I had finally unpacked my belongings in a comfortable cabin in *Terror*. I had tracked down the stuff I had left on *Crane*, when I had to leave her suddenly to go with *Modeste* to Borneo. It had travelled up to Hong Kong and back, and was now in *Terror's* baggage room. I was now hurriedly packing, during the middle of the night, to join *Modeste* yet again, this time in rather a fragile post 'run ashore' state. It did seem as if I could only join the ship in some kind of emergency. The phone then rang. 'Doc', the staff man said, '*Modeste* is at sea at the moment, on her way back from Pulau Tioman. She will be at Johore Shoal Buoy at 11am. I'll let you know soon how we're going to get you out to her.' The phone rang again. 'The tug *Enigma* is going out to meet *Modeste* at 11am', the duty man said, 'she's taking some emergency things they will be short of. You can join *Enigma* in the dockyard.' By now I was quite recovered, all thoughts of a stay in *Terror* forgotten. What was about to happen sounded more interesting.

It was a beautiful morning when I went down to the dockyard. The tug was not the fastest of vessels and it took three hours to go down the now familiar Straits of Johore. The air was full of the sweet scent of vegetation and, as the master of the tug invited me to join him on his bridge, I had a wonderful view of the nearby Johore jungle. The master had a glass of whisky on his chart table. The bottle was balanced beside it, quite safely as the water was so calm. I declined his invitation to join him in a dram and we had an interesting talk on the way down to the buoy. At 11am, we met *Modeste* and I was pleased that I got a loud cheer when they saw that I was joining them. I was able to board this time by climbing over their rail from the tug, which allowed me the odd crack about preferring this method to trusting my fate to their jackstay transfer skills: last time, on the way to Borneo, I got soaked. *Enigma*'s crew man passed over the stores and we left at once, supposedly for Ceylon, although this was to present a problem.

Modeste's crew knew that she was shortly to leave the Far East, but this sudden departure meant disappointment for many of the ship's company, and more than one heart wrenching farewell had to be cancelled. From my point of view, however, there was no problem.

We were accompanied from Singapore by a destroyer. The arrival of warships on their doorstep made the government of Ceylon nervous, especially as, for some reason, we were not allowed to disclose our destination. They would not allow us refuel in any of their ports, so we had to use a British RFA, the *Arndale*. We had left Singapore so hurriedly that we had no eggs, fresh fruit or vegetables and supplies of tinned foods were running low. In addition to refusing us fuel, Ceylon also refused us permission to stock up on food. The Bay of Bengal produced a steady roll, just enough to need lee-boards on the bunks. This was in contrast to the next leg of our unexpected journey, the long haul across the Arabian Sea. This was very rough all the way.

As we went through the Straits of Hormuz and into the Persian Gulf, I was given a new task. Instead of being a member of the crypto team and then the 'fall of shot' recorder as on *Crane*, I was made *Modeste*'s intelligence officer. This sounded very grand, and the captain started in the usual way. 'Doc, you've nothing to do', he said. 'I want you to become our Intelligence Officer. You can have access to both logs, that is the one which holds the routine signals, and the classified one, that is the secret one. Read them through every day, and then brief us all in the Operations Room every morning at 11am.' So I found myself reading signals from the MOD in London, appreciations from British Embassies in the region and from 'observers' on the ground. From these sources, I had to prepare a daily appreciation of what was happening in Iraq and the Gulf. I found it very funny that here I was, a newcomer to the Navy, giving a daily briefing to professional naval officers. I informed them one morning, for example, that the Shat al Arab, the main waterway into Iraq, and eventually Baghdad, had been blocked by the sinking of two barges. The briefings stopped when it was clear that, as in Borneo and Celebes, the situation had calmed down. This seemed par for the course, but we were at least there if British nationals required protection.

I thoroughly enjoyed the period that followed. From the Arabian Sea we went into the Persian Gulf via the Gulf of Oman, the temperature rising all the way. It was high summer in a region which is always hot, the cabins reaching a hundred degrees and the boiler and engine rooms reaching a hundred and thirty. Unlike the two permanent Gulf frigates, we had no air conditioning. The sea temperature was only a little lower, which probably accounted for the fantastic sea creatures one could see in the Gulf of Oman. They were so numerous, and the water so clear, it was like looking down into a nightmarish kind of minestrone. There were long sea snakes, porpoises, sharks, and fish of all sizes and brilliant colours. Amongst them I recognised rays, groupers, snappers and marlin. There were catfish with poisonous 'whiskers', huge jellyfish, garfish with long snouts, and barracuda. These were all in such great numbers, and the water so clear, that there was a three-dimensional effect. That is there appeared to be layer upon layer of fish. Perhaps it was not surprising that, with all the predators present, no flying fish were seen. In fact, I did not remember seeing any west of Ceylon.

A VIP came on board and gave us an idea of our future plans. The situation in Iraq having settled down, other employment had been found for us. After a quick call at Bahrain we were to carry out anti-gun-running patrols off the Muscat coast. This was to 'maintain good political relations with the smaller Gulf states', which meant Muscat and Oman. The small armed forces of these countries were 'advised' by British army officers on secondment. The names of those forces were wonderful, such as 'The Sultan of Muscat's Armed Forces' and 'The Trucial Oman Scouts'. It was interesting to see how Britain keeps an eye on the main chance.

The VIP inspected the ship's company, hastily drawn up on deck. He came to an able seaman who was in the early stages of growing a beard. In the Navy, this requires permission, the man in question requiring to ask the captain for 'permission to grow'. The visitor asked the seaman how long he had been growing and was surprised by the quick answer 'All me life, sir!' *Modeste* was due home, as we knew, and I would leave her in Aden. How I was to return to the Far East was as yet undecided. Modeste would call at Aqaba on the Red Sea on the way home, 'to show support for our troops in Jordan'. Again the MOD was not going to miss a trick.

I met one of the two doctors on the Gulf frigates. They were pretty bored, never went anywhere, and very envious of my travels in the Far East. *Modeste* set off on anti-smuggling and anti-gunrunning patrols, which involved stopping and searching small dhows. Our sailors were armed ostentatiously for this task, and much enjoyed the change of work. For a short time we carried two 'good' dhow skippers to help generally and with the Arabic in particular.

All along the Gulf coast, we could see how people tried to minimise the heat in their homes. Their houses were built with wide square 'chimneys' in the centre, so that hot air was convected up and out. I visited a heat exhaustion emergency treatment caravan on the jetty at Bahrain, where we called in briefly. It was kept at a temperature of seventy degrees, which felt like walking into a deep freeze.

By far the most remarkable vessel we stopped was not a dhow, but an open-decked boat about sixty feet long. On board, there were two hundred and seven people, crammed together with no shelter from the sun. We were told by our interpreters that they were pilgrims from Kuwait bound for Karachi, but that seemed doubtful. They had no weapons with them and we gave them water, sugar and cigarettes. Their faces were those of Biblical illustrations, usually bearded. Many wore Arab headdress. One old man came to their ship's rail, which was on a level with ours. He had cellulitis of a hand. I gave him antibiotics but, even after prolonged conversation with one of our

Modeste approaches 'pilgrim ship' in Persian Gulf

dhow people, I remained doubtful if he had any idea how they were to be taken. As their craft pushed off from *Modeste's* side in the middle of the Gulf, he was still gazing at the little yellow tablets in his hand.

Many of the dhows we stopped were filthy. Many carried sheep, goats and donkeys. Women were few, heavily veiled, and usually dressed in black. One dhow contained one of the seven Sheiks of Trucial Oman, or so it was said. He was seated in some style in the stern of his boat, with three women and a transistor radio.

Everyone looked forward to a day off, and it came when we anchored early one morning at the small uninhabited island of Halul, off the eastern tip of Qatar. As many as could be spared went ashore for a banyan, or barbecue. We spent the day eating and swimming from the coral sand beach, the sand being too hot to stand on with bare feet. The captain stayed on board and lent me his snorkel and flippers, which made my day. Just off the beach, there were numerous coral reefs with many brightly coloured fish of all sizes. With the snorkel, I could just laze on the surface, watching fish for long periods. The sea was a faint blue colour and crystal clear, with only a ripple on the surface. A parrot fish I saw had a beak just like that of its namesake. We kept a close eye open for less desirable fishy phenomena as, on the way into the beach, we had seen a manta ray and barracuda. This day off was a wonderful change from the stifling conditions on board ship.

This being the Royal Navy, nothing was allowed to interfere with the requirement for each ship to carry out a General Drill once during each commission. So the fact that we were in the Persian Gulf in response to a political emergency was a non-issue. Nor did it matter that it was the hottest month of the year and we had no air conditioning. The latter fact was to land me, if not actually in trouble, then pretty close to it. Certainly I found myself subject to a slightly raised executive eyebrow. General Drill is designed to test a ship's ability to cope with any situation it may encounter. This ability is a valued and valuable Royal Navy tradition.

For this particular exercise, Captain F, the senior officer in the squadron, came aboard and ordered a series of 'evolutions' to be carried out without warning. These evolutions are not always serious, but designed to test ingenuity. Past examples include 'Fry an egg six feet in front of the bows,' this occurring while the ship was travelling at ten knots. This had meant lashing appropriate lengths of spar into position and sending one of the cooks out to perch on this precarious platform with his equipment. On another occasion, Captain F suddenly threw his cap into the sea, started a stop watch and said 'Right! That's a man overboard. Rescue him!' Other squadron officers usually accompany their senior officer to assess their various specialties. As will be seen, however, *St Brides Bay* was called upon, on two occasions, to carry out evolutions more dramatic than any likely to be laid on for General Drill.

The ship was dealing well with this year's General Drill when Captain F announced on the ship's broadcast, 'D'ye hear there? The ventilation in the engine room and boiler room has failed. The ventilation in the engine room and boiler room has failed.' At the same time he got someone to switch off the relevant fans. Before starting this evolution, the temperature in these compartments was in the hundred and twenty degree area. It struck me that to switch off these fans was asking for trouble, drill or no drill. After a short interval, I went down the ladders to see how the men were getting on. They had organised themselves into ten minute watches, but even that was too long. I thought that this was ridiculous, so, taking a deep breath, I went up to the bridge. Captain F was leaning on the rail talking to the captain of *Modeste*. I delivered my say, and he replied in three words: 'Thank you, doctor.' I then withdrew.

Later in the day, the time arrived for an inspection of the Medical Department. In spite of repeated jokey remarks along the lines of, 'You just have to inspect yourself, ha! ha!,' I realised that Captain F was to inspect the sick bay and the SBA himself. The sick bay threw up no problems, but the next bit did. 'Rig the wardroom as an operating theatre. The PO cook is suffering from appendicitis and is to lie on the operating table. Have the butcher mark Macburney's Point in black.' Macburney's Point is a surface landmark for localising the position of the appendix. I was still angry at what I thought was a stupid game with the engine room fans, and told the SBA not to open the sterile towels and instruments but to put the drums intact on the table. I did not see any point in opening them for what after all was only a game. The cook and the butcher were summoned and played their parts with better grace than I did. I discussed Macburney's Point with Captain F who seemed very proud of his knowledge. He said nothing untoward about the rather half-hearted medical aspect of his inspection, but he got his own back later. In the report on the ship's performance during its General Drill, he included the paragraph: 'MEDICAL DEPARTMENT. This department was well organised. It did, however, seem a little unwilling to descend to the level of General Drill.' I could only agree!

Events were moving, it seemed, at speed. The next incident was described in a letter:

> This is the hottest time of the year in the Gulf. The effort required to do anything, even writing this letter, is very great. The temperature rarely falls below 90° and there is seldom even a slight breeze. Everyone is covered in prickly heat and three days ago I had a real medical emergency. He was a stoker who, his mates volunteered, had not been taking the salt tablets we had provided for everyone on board. I thought he was suffering from extreme salt deficiency, with associated deficiency of fluid due to the extreme heat, and he was certainly very ill. He seemed about to die, there being no recordable pulse or blood pressure. He was unconscious when carried in to the sick bay. With intravenous saline and plasma substitute he eventually regained consciousness. The drip was a somewhat Heath Robinson affair, the 'drip stand' being a broom handle wedged in the gimbals of the upper bunk. The amount of saline and plasma expander he received was calculated at random, there obviously being no lab facilities available. He is now much better, fully conscious, and he should do well. One of the Gulf Frigates had just lost a stoker with the same condition, although they are beautifully air conditioned.

From the Gulf we travelled down to Aden, also hot, although we passed through a cold patch on the way south. The temperature fell to sixty-two degrees and ventilation fans were quickly turned off. I now left *Modeste* and waited in Aden until *St Brides Bay* arrived. I was sorry to see the *Modeste* crew head home, having had a lot of fun with them. It was good of them to send me a copy of their commission magazine when they reached the UK.

11

Aden and the Blue Peter

HMS *Sheba* is to Aden what *Tamar* is to Hong Kong, and *Terror* is to Singapore – that is a 'stone frigate'. This was to be the fifth of the kind that I had lived in since joining up, in addition to the real frigates of *Crane*, *Modeste* and *St Brides Bay*. *Modeste* had by now headed home and I realised how a stateless person must feel. *Sheba* was very small, with only five officers, but it had the best food so far, cooked by a Yemeni. There was considerable anti-British feeling in Aden, which explained the wire netting covering the open windows. This was to prevent the 'playful' locals repeating the previous month's attempt to lob in hand grenades. There was also a great deal of barbed wire on the walls and an armed sentry at the gate. The latter was a 'locally entered' Somali, which meant he wore a naval rating's uniform but had the cap replaced by a red tarboosh, a fez-like hat. He was very black, very smart and altogether a splendid sight. He was, of course, a Muslim like the other locally entered ratings. On one occasion the CO of *Sheba*, normally a mild-tempered man, was having a bad day probably due to the extra work resulting from the emergency in Iraq. Unable to find his locally-entered assistant, a usually ever-present and conscientious man – the conversation proceeded as follows: 'Where's that … Ali?' said the CO. 'Saying his prayers, sir,' came the response.' This caused a spluttering of rage, and then, 'So is … Christopher Robin! Get him here! NOW!'

As there was, for the time being, no ship of the squadron in Aden, I had no regular work to do and instead found myself occupied with a variety of other tasks. These included counting East African pounds in large numbers, the wherewithal with which to pay the other ranks of the Kenyan navy. Of more importance, however, I was again involved in coding and decoding signals. One night, during the early hours, I found myself decoding an urgent signal from John Hare, the UK Minister of Defence, which outlined the classified up-to-date contingency plans for evacuating British citizens from various places in the Gulf and Middle East. Decoding this presented no problems but I was then supposed to re-encode this message and send it on to the C in C Middle East. At this point, I was acutely aware of how embryonic my crypto skills were. I therefore put discretion before valour and wakened a real naval officer to pass the message on. I explained to him that my carrying out the task might be equivalent to publishing this secret information in the Aden daily newspaper. He did not seem to mind, although I felt a bit guilty for having disturbed his slumber.

The lack of work gave me time again to consider what I was going to do when the time came to finish national service. I had more or less narrowed the options down to general medicine or general practice, but the idea of a permanent career in the Navy was still an option. As there was no hurry, I put off a decision for the meantime.

Various interesting people passed through *Sheba* during this fortnight. They included two ferry pilots who had flown out planes for the carrier *Bulwark*. She had just lost one on take off, when its braking parachute opened accidentally. The aircraft hit the sea about 500 yards (1500 ft) ahead of the carrier, which just missed it by going hard a-starboard. The rescue helicopter then found that its winch would not work, and the pilot was eventually picked up by sea boat. He escaped with minor facial injuries.

A Queen's Messenger spent the night on *Sheba*. A retired naval captain, he was responsible for carrying the British diplomatic bag between Aden and Addis Ababa or Khartoum. Also spending some time in Aden, for rest and recreation, was the East African Navy's inshore minesweeper *Bassingham*. Her three officers, who were British, enjoyed the relative comfort and the food of *Sheba*. Incidentally, I discovered in *Sheba* that I had a more than average liking for potatoes. 'Ishmael, can I have some more potatoes, please?' I found myself saying repeatedly. A Cantonese steward on one of the frigates had taught me the phrase *'teemsing suzai?'* which means roughly the same. Living in the dry heat of Aden was not really an enjoyable experience. Swimming was possible at the Gold Mohur Club, behind shark nets, but like all areas of Aden that I saw, it was hot, dusty and somewhat flyblown. This part of the town lay on a narrow coastal strip with a backdrop of barren, brown mountains, with no greenery anywhere. The Crescent was the only shopping street and the hotel of that name the only one of good standing. Street traders invited passers-by in for a *shufti*. Arab women looked like upturned black vases, their view of the world limited to what they could see through a small meshed opening in their hoods.

While at Aden, I had to go on board the RFA *Wave Premier* to 'inspect her tanks'. What possible purpose this served, I did not discover, but climbing down the long ladders into the tanks was very eerie. I also had to go on board the *Strathnaver* to decide, with the ship's master, what to do with a sick naval rating they had on board. The ship carried two doctors who, although it was eight o'clock in the morning, immediately offered me a whisky and soda. They had just been up all night with a heat stroke case, and were having a busy time all round. The biggest difference from our tiny sick bays was the presence of two attractive nursing sisters.

In due course *St Brides Bay* arrived and, just after I had moved aboard her, we had an exciting five days at sea. It started with *St Brides* flying the Blue Peter. This is a flag flown when a ship is about to sail unexpectedly and all crew ashore are expected to rejoin urgently. It is a rectangular blue flag with a white rectangle in the middle. The Army and the RAF helped by patrolling the streets with loudspeakers, bringing back those they found to the ship. We left Aden in great haste, only three men short. In spite of being alongside the wall, we had to leave with less water than we wanted because of a strike of dock workers. This meant that water was available for only half an hour, morning and afternoon. As showers were not possible, and everyone was suffering from prickly heat, this was a pity. The reason for *St Brides* hurried departure was that our recent acquaintance, the East African Navy's *Bassingham*, had got into serious trouble. The little inshore minesweeper had left Aden five days previously, en route to her base at Mombasa in Kenya. She had lost power in heavy seas and had requested help. We were nearest and hence rushed to her rescue. We crossed the Gulf of Aden and found her halfway between the island of Socotra and Cape Guardafui in Somalia, the northeast tip of the Horn of Africa. The seas were heavy and must have been frightening on such a small craft. They were greatly relieved to see us, having had no sleep for three days, and they told us that a great cheer had gone up when they spotted us.

Their ship looked a mess, battered and scraped as it was and at one point they thought it had gone beneath them. We got them aboard with difficulty and the *St Brides* ratings looked after their opposite numbers brilliantly. The fifteen African ratings were given an enormous meal and I heard great merriment coming from Five Mess, where they were temporarily accommodated. I put their engineer officer, who had fallen down a hatch, in the sick bay with a suspected cracked vertebra and exhaustion. Until the sea went down a little, *Bassingham* was lashed to our leeside with everything that could be used as a fender being wedged between the two ships. A volunteer crew from *Brides* then boarded her and we towed her back to Aden, with her own crew taking over for the last stage. On the way back, I had a closer look at Cape Guardafui. Dark, desolate mountains rose straight out of the sea. It was a great shame that this happened to be such an unattractive place but at least I had *seen* Africa, for what it was worth.

Happily our stay in Aden was not prolonged further and it was a relief to be out at sea again. We returned to the coast of Muscat and were looking forward to more anti-gunrunning patrols, when the unexpected occurred. Once again, a signal changed everything.

12

Collision at sea

We arrived off Muscat to take part in an operation with *Bulwark*. She was to fly off her aircraft against Talib's rebels in Oman, who had recently acquired new arms by smuggling them in via dhows. Britain had undertaken to protect the Sultan of Oman from the Talib and this was the smuggling we had been helping to guard against before we set out for Aden. Just as the operation started, however, we got orders to return to our own part of the world, the Far East. Our place with *Bulwark* was to be taken, as was more appropriate, by one of the Gulf frigates. This was probably a welcome change for them.

Twelve hours later we received a signal telling us that there had been a serious collision between two oil tankers off the entrance to the Persian Gulf. Early reports mentioned bodies in the sea and several men were said to be badly burned at some location. Any ship in the area carrying a doctor was requested to attend. The burned men were from the tanker *Melika*, which was close to *Bulwark* and so was looked after by her. We were therefore no longer required from the medical standpoint, but were sent to help the second vessel, the *Ferdinand Gilabert,* a French tanker from Dunkirk. She was said to be on fire and had been abandoned.

We were the first ship to reach her and a sorry sight she was. The falls from the davits hung loose, the boats having left. A rope ladder hung over her

The abandoned tanker, Ferdinand Gilabert, *before boarding
by* St Brides Bay's *fire-fighting party*

Fire-fighting party on the smoke-blackened tanker's bridge. The fire is now under control

stern at an odd angle, suggesting haste. Her bows were undercut and missing for thirty feet at a height of a few feet above the sea, where she had risen over the bigger *Melika's* well deck. The remaining upper part of her bows were angled downwards and creaked as she rose and fell with the swell. The bow appeared to be close to breaking off completely. Flames crackled on her bridge, producing clouds of smoke. The superstructure was blackened and there was a smell of burning paint and oil.

St Brides' captain had to make a decision. It seemed that no men were left on the tanker and, thus, the question was simply whether we would be able to do anything about the fire. He decided that, to assess the situation, he had to send a small party across. Five ratings under the command of a young sub-lieutenant went over in the motorboat. They made for the ship's stern and the dangling rope ladder. Unfortunately the tanker's rudder and the large single screw were coming clear of the water every time she pitched. As the rope ladder entered the sea close to these, it was impossible for the motorboat to get near enough. A big swell was running but the sub-lieutenant tied a rope around his waist and swam to the foot of the ladder. He managed to make it, hoping, as he commented later, that the ladder would stay secured up top. It did. He quickly got his men and their fire fighting equipment on board, and the motorboat was able to lie-off in the charge of its coxswain. The fire proved to be less dramatic than it had looked from afar and was eventually brought under control by this small party. The owners of the stricken ship must have wondered, in spite of the fire and the damaged bow, if their crew had been too quick to abandon ship. The situation on the tanker was now stable. She was drifting without power and with no crew, and was therefore a 'danger to shipping'. The emphasis, which had first been on giving medical help, and then on fire-fighting, changed yet again. Salvage and salvage money!

The rules governing salvage of a drifting, unmanned ship state that the first ship to get a line on board her is the first to benefit from any salvage award. We were first on the scene, although we realised that others were fast heading our way. It was, therefore, necessary to establish a tow as soon as possible. The motorboat quickly returned from the tanker, being urgently required to take across the salvage crew that was put together from the various departments. This included a signalman, engineers and seamen. The first question was, would she stay afloat, and the second, could we establish a tow? The answer to the first was 'Yes, probably' as she was a tanker, and to the second, 'You bet.'

There was a hairy moment as the boat returned for the salvage crew. A high sea was running and we had moved into the tanker's lee to make recovery of the boat easier. The tanker was, therefore, upwind of us and, because of sea and wind conditions, drifting down on us faster than we were getting out of her way. The motorboat was thus between the two ships, in a space closing fast. It was in imminent danger of being crushed as it slowed down to 'hook on'. It only just managed this task before the captain had to give the emergency order, 'Full ahead both engines.' Even then it was a bit dodgy, as one of the hoists jammed and the boat was barely clear of the water when we shot off. Some of the men thought the situation so risky that they actually climbed the falls rather than wait for the boat to be pulled up. All went well in the end, but the slightly shaken captain told me that this was the first time in the commission that he had given this order. Normally, Royal Navy practice is to order the number of revolutions rather than use the terms: 'slow', 'half' and 'full-ahead' or 'astern'. There was discussion in the wardroom later as to whether this risky situation could have been avoided. It was concluded that the captain had no option but to act as he did. The state of the sea was such that it had been necessary to help our boat by 'giving her a lee'. The wardroom also decided that the young *St. Brides'* officer, who had led the fire-fighting party, had done a good job.

History repeated itself for me at this point. This time it was the navigator who said 'Doc, you've nothing to do .We're going to try to get a wire across to her to take her in tow. I've got to write the report on the operation but I'm going to be busy, so will you do it for me?' I said I would, but was not familiar with the technical language such a report would require. 'That's OK. Keep a log of everything that happens, and the times, and then write it all up in your own words. We'll go over it later and I'll put in the jargon.' So I wrote the log of the operation and also the outline of the salvage report. One year later, I received a cheque for £60, a lieutenant's share of the salvage award.

The first attempt to establish a tow was unsuccessful. The motorboat was at the limit of its capability because of the weather, and only a few men went

Left: Crisis! The twist in the fo'ard falls can be seen

Below: Showing damage to tanker's bow

Fire-fighting party returning to St Brides Bay

Showing damage to tanker's bow

across in it before it had to be brought inboard. The coxswain then tried to fire a Coston gun line across, but it was repeatedly blown away by a rising wind. Eventually he was successful and a wire hawser was attached on our quarterdeck to the gun line. But the hawser was too heavy for the few men on the damaged ship to pull out of the sea. The tanker was, of course, without power and therefore could not use her winches.

The captain now made a daring decision. He decided to lay our ship alongside the well deck of the tanker, her lowest point. He calculated that her height above the sea there would be pretty close to the height above the sea of the highest part of our forecastle. Volunteers were asked for on the ship's broadcast. They were to clamber over when the ships came together, the idea being that the extra men would provide enough pulling power to get the towing hawser out of the sea and up on to the tanker.

The next bit was exciting. Our plan worked at a cost, happily not of life, but it was certainly dangerous. Coming in with our port side to, the first approach failed and we had to back off. The second time our approach was just right and the tanker's side towered above us as we went in. The problem, which we had previously not appreciated, now became obvious. The roll of each ship was different in frequency and there were several loud crashes as the ships rolled heavily against each other. Our bow was bent for about twenty feet and rivets were sprung. The starboard side of our forecastle deck was buckled for thirty feet and compartments in the bows were flooded. One of the ship's main frame members was later found to have been broken. The motorboat, after its previous escape and the service it had given earlier, was now completely destroyed, crushed with a loud and horrible splintering sound between its davits and the tanker's side. At this point, I heard someone shouting 'The depth charges! The depth charges!' which were just aft of where the ships were in contact at each roll. It transpired that the detonators had been removed and there was apparently no risk. I heard someone laughing hysterically over the high background noise.

Men had been waiting on the forecastle with protective clothing and the odd grip containing food. I watched from the safety of the bridge as they timed their jumps in the wet, noisy semi-darkness. They threw their bags and some tools over, chose their moment as the ships crashed together; and jumped.

About twenty men went over. Looking down into the awful space between the rolling ships was bad enough. Crossing the gap took guts.

The extra pulling power meant that the heavy hawser could now be lifted on to the tanker, fed through the 'bull ring' in her bow, and made fast. The collision had happened to the east of Ras-al-Had, the most easterly point of Oman. The nearest proper port was Karachi and we set off to tow her in that direction. But we could make no progress. The tanker was too heavy for us to tow in that sea, and the situation was made worse by the 'steering effect' of the damaged bow. Attempts to tow her stern first were also unsuccessful. After nine hours crawling at a few knots through the darkness, the tow eventually parted, taking our last strong hawser with it.

Loch Killisport, one of the Gulf frigates, came out from the Gulf and we went to help *Bulwark* with the other tanker *Melika,* still afloat thirty miles away. This ship, a much more modern tanker, was listing so heavily to port that the sea was washing continually over her rail. Jets of water, forced out of the circular openings of her tanks, shot high in the air with each roll. Her walkway along the well decks was sheared away where the other tanker's bows had sliced over her. The remnants of catwalk and piping protruded over the side at each end of the cut. This episode showed how difficult it is to sink an empty tanker. Internally these ships are designed to carry large volumes of liquid cargo and it follows that whether this is oil or sea water makes no difference.

Eventually we were detached to have our damage repaired back in Singapore. As we left, the sea had gone right down and both tankers were being towed to Karachi. Two ships were used to tow each tanker. They included *Loch Killisport, Bulwark,* the destroyer *Puma* and one other.

So what did we achieve? We only displace 1,500 tons, but at least we kept the 10,000 ton *Ferdinand Gilabert* stable and under control for twenty-four hours, long enough to allow more powerful ships to arrive. Our presence removed the danger to other shipping presented by an unlit, drifting hulk. We extinguished a fire, which might have spread, and provided the salvage crew who took her all the way to Karachi. The ship's company learned a lot about boat and ship handling, and seamanship generally, from this dramatic event. We acquired three souvenirs: the ship's brass bell, and two tortoises. These

*The other tanker involved, Malika, lies awash on her port side. The walkway
has been carried away by Ferdinand Gilabert's bows*

now 'belonged' to *St Brides* and were imaginatively named 'Ferdinand' and 'Gilabert'.

One of our engine room artificers gave me one of *St Brides* sprung rivets. This was hammered into the bow when the ship was built, and should have remained there until she was scrapped. The ERA mounted the rivet as a paperweight on a piece of polished brass shell cap. It was a splendid reminder of an exciting event.

13

Ceylon and return to the Far East

It was good to be heading east once again. I found I had extra jobs to do, including running the wardroom wine fund, in place of one of the salvage team on the tanker, and teaching basic school subjects to those who needed them for 'advancement', which means promotion. I also had an alarmingly keen first aid class. We made landfall on the Indian coast at Goa but did not enter. This was at one time a Portuguese settlement and was full of shipping. Later, as we travelled south, we had good views of the coast of Travancore and the mountains known as the Western Ghats.

Radio Ceylon made amusing listening. 'Have you booked your seats for *The Ten Commandments*? If not, get them from … ' The request programme continued, 'Now here is *Down by the Riverside* for Mr. Jinnamatami of Kandy.' There was a long pause, and then a crash, before the scratchy record began.

This time there was no problem about getting clearance to enter Ceylon. We called in at Trincomalee to take on fuel. There seemed little point in going ashore as we were at a bare fuelling jetty, with only a few red-roofed buildings present against a backdrop of thick green jungle. The few notice boards still standing were in Tamil, but there were no signs of life and obviously the great days of 'Trinco' were over. It used to be a frequent stopping place for Royal Navy ships.

Approaching oil fuel depot, Trincomalee

On bridge of St Brides Bay *– note Captain's chair and covered chart table*

Nonetheless we were to be here for two hours, so I sneaked ashore, seeing our damage from shore-side for the first time. It was impressive. I wandered off behind the deserted jetty into partially cleared jungle. As I was walking through this clearing, I saw ten large men in grey boiler suits sitting watching me from the top of an oil storage tank. This was odd, I thought. What could they be doing in such a place? Suddenly I realised the large 'men in boiler suits of unusual colour' were, in fact, large monkeys, but I did not know of what kind. They got up and raced away as I approached. They were probably harmless, but to come on them so unexpectedly was disconcerting. I also saw two very large green beetles rolling a pellet of sheep dung along the sand. In the short time I had ashore, Ceylon seemed similar to Borneo with many bright birds and butterflies.

On the way back from Trincomalee to Singapore, the captain asked me to neuter his cat, Harvey. The operation went well but as he was a very keen cat lover I thought it politic to keep the beast in the sick bay for twenty-four hours. The LSBA and I continued to give it its usual diet of flying fish and tinned milk. For the operation, the cat was placed on its back on a splint and secured with a broad crepe bandage. I gave it plenty of local anaesthetic and

"ALL READY TO OPERATE, REDFORD ??"

St Brides Bay, *Bay of Bengal. The operation on the Captain's cat* it did not appear to feel a thing, not even the two stitches. The event led to a hilarious cartoon on the ship's notice board, showing me waving a huge knife and shouting 'Ready to operate, Redford?' The LSBA is grinning behind a surgical mask and Harvey looks totally unconcerned as he lies under a big theatre lamp. This cartoon was reproduced in the ship's end-of-commission magazine of which I was again to receive a copy. This time the drawing was accompanied by a footnote by the first lieutenant. I thought his biological education must have been slightly neglected, as it read, 'Harvey undergoes transition to Henrietta, thanks to the doctor's successful efforts.'

The Malacca Straits are beautiful at night during fine weather. As before, the heady smell of the Malayan jungle came out over the sea, and there was the occasional flash of a lighthouse on the Sumatran coast. This was my fourth trip through these straits and, as we headed back to Singapore, my eighth through the equally beautiful Johore Strait. I was again, as they say, 'glad that I had joined'. And there was, it turned out, still more to come!

St Brides Bay headed straight into dry dock to have her damage repaired and we moved back to the comfort and good food of *Terror*. I now had the luxury of a single cabin. The stuff I left there on the day of my hurried departure for the Middle East was covered in mildew, just as had been the case with luggage brought here from *Crane* after my equally hurried departure to Borneo.

The surgeon captain in *Terror* asked to see me. This was the first I knew that such a person existed. 'Ah, yes,' he said, 'you've been in the Gulf in August. Pretty awful there at that time of year.' I agreed, and we discussed the medical facilities available in the Gulf, in Bahrain and in Aden, I was about to leave when he dropped a bombshell. 'By the way' he said '*Crane* is going on a cruise to New Zealand and Australia later in the year, and she will be showing the flag at a couple of Pacific islands on the way. You'll be going with her.'

This was stunning news! I heard that it was the Captain F – he of the General Drill – who recommended I go on this cruise. He thought, I was told, that I had had a hard time by spending two spells in the Persian Gulf area, with *Modeste* and then *St Brides,* everybody else having done only one. I was amazed, considering that if this was true, it had not occurred to me and, in any case, I had really enjoyed my time in the Middle East. There was still the possibility that the Quemoy fighting might cause this Pacific cruise to be cancelled, although this was said to be unlikely. I crossed my fingers. With an attractive, three-month cruise to the Pacific lined up, it was hardly surprising that the intervening period in Singapore and Hong Kong was rather less exciting.

Apart from medical guard duties, I had one new job, this time without the usual preliminaries. The vast amount of commercial shipping arriving at Singapore's main harbour, that is the harbour on the south side of the island, was thought to present an attractive target for terrorists. It was decided to simulate such an attack, with naval frogmen playing the part of the enemy. They were to carry out an attack in the hours of darkness on a given night. I was told that I would be 'Diving Safety Officer' for the frogmen, which made me think hard and hurry to read the text books. During the event, I spent the night trying to sleep on a coil of rope on the deck of a small fishing boat. I did see the attackers twice in the water, but they were in mid-harbour at the time and just how successful they were I did not hear. Happily, they did not need my services.

St Bride's damage was quickly repaired and I joined her once again for my third visit to Hong Kong. It seemed only yesterday that I had arrived there for the first time. This time the emphasis was on regular patrolling around both the island and the mainland area of the colony, the aim being to prevent abduction of fishermen into Red China, an occurrence which had been on the increase. Although Hong Kong is British, the Communist Chinese claim the waters just outside the city, and we had spotted the occasional Chinese warship.

We anchored every night for a week at Castle Peak Bay. Castle Peak is a sort of Chinese Gourdon – a fishing village on Scotland's north-east coast – to which junks arrive every evening to unload their catch. Mostly, these are powered by sail and they are much more elegant than our seine net boats. They are not so cumbersome to handle as they appear and I found them very fascinating. Each is operated by a family, the wife doing most of the hard work, hoisting sails and so on. The husband looks after the nets, which are often made of nylon. There are many children on board, as there are ashore. These fishing people knew why an RN ship was around, and seemed pleased to see us. We went ashore and had a splendid view over the frontier into Red China. Naval personnel are forbidden from approaching the frontier gate.

On the bridge of St Brides Bay. *Note binnacle and framework for awning*

*Lookout on port wing of bridge, St Brides Bay. Just as well for
him the ship was at anchor at this time!*

There was time for a proper look at Hong Kong. It is both very wealthy and very poor. The area around the ferry terminal on the Kowloon side has many expensive shops, and the world-famous Peninsula Hotel. We had tea there one afternoon and felt transported back in time to the days of the Raj. Punkah fans spun gently over cane armchairs and waiters moved quietly about, dressed in peculiar old-style costume. Tea consisted of traditional delicate sandwiches and freshly baked scones and cakes.

The upmarket area of central Victoria contained equally famous night spots, such as Jimmy's Kitchen, Maxim's and the Cafe de Chine. The first port of call for all Royal Navy men arriving in Hong Kong was Jack Conder's, a bar run by an ex-Royal Navy man, and famous for its club sandwiches. Also in Kowloon, but less grand, were the Bombay, Luigi's, Mary Wong's, the Princes Gardens, the Bamboo, the New Mandarin and many others. The real heart of Hong Kong, however, is Wanchai, and we spent much of our off-time in this purely Chinese area of the city. This may sound odd when ninety-eight percent of the population was Chinese, but there were areas, centred on Wanchai, where non-Chinese were not seen. Most of these areas were out of bounds to Service personnel, which was a pity as they were fascinating and different from the cosmopolitan area.

The best way to see Wanchai, we found, was to walk around its streets in the evening. These streets were the only home to many, not just down-and-outs as in Western cities, but whole families. Some slept on the pavement and others bedded down for the night in cardboard boxes. Other families lived day and night on their tiny sampans. Food was to be had from 'The Stalls', cooked over braziers in the street, hence the typical smell of Wanchai. People clustered round these stalls, children passing urine unconcernedly in the gutter. Cripples abounded, some healthy children apparently were maltreated in infancy to suit them for this mode of life. Some had bizarre prostheses, for example a three-legged stool used as an artificial foot for a man who had had a leg amputated at the knee. It was like a scene from Hogarth. There were people everywhere, particularly on Saturday nights. Rickshaw men, who live short lives, touted for business, as did the persuasive individuals outside the many nightclubs and bars. Streetwise urchins crowded the doors of these places, imploring, 'Come in, sir. You like *very* nice girl, sir?' The bars included the Arizona, of earlier incident, the China Nights, the Lucky Man, and the Skyroom. As in central Victoria, the clack of mah-jong pieces was to be heard as one walked down the streets. There were little shops given over to this game, open-fronted, as the nights were warm. Most of Wanchai's little shops were similarly open to the air and the passers-by.

We tried Chinese opera at the Hong Kong Grand Theatre in spite of the warning given by the man at the door. 'All Chinese, sir' he said, and he was right. It was difficult to buy tickets for what was definitely not an entertainment intended for Westerners. The audience of families, who brought along their babies, were amused to see us. The performance was day-long, with families wandering in and out, talking to one another, reading newspapers and drinking lemonade. This whole scene took place against what was, to my ears, the continuous dreadful noise of the opera. This performance was called *One Hundred Thousand Men Tramp the Jade Pass*. The orchestra sat on the stage to the left, in open necked shirts. There was one violin, two saxophones, one 'flute' and two Chinese-type double basses. Following each sentence uttered, there was a loud clanging of a gong and cymbals, repeated also at each exit and entrance. We found it difficult to identify any coordination between the music and the singing. The actors were all dressed in bright silk costumes and funny hats, one of which had two snakes for ears, which the wearer kept whisking about. There seemed to be few laughs in a mixture of song and dialogue with much coy byplay. The sceneshifters, in vests and trousers, walked on and off in the midst of the action, taking ages to reset the scenery with grave deliberation. The actors ignored them, continuing to perform around them. One scenery man kept peeping at the audience from behind a pillar. We stayed for one hour.

The ship now undertook Indigo patrols, that is looking for smugglers and abductors, in the Tolo Harbour area. This is a wide natural harbour located amongst many islands in the New Territories. This exercise finished after a week and I decided to take a few days leave and go on my own to Macao.

Macao, or Macau, is a mirror image of Hong Kong only it belongs to Portugal. In other words, it is a small colony on the mainland of China. Macao and Hong Kong sit on opposite sides of the estuary of the Pearl river, about

Junks at Macao. Mountains of communist China in background

forty miles apart. It is a free port with a reputation for gold smuggling. I went on the ferry 'Tai Ling', about which a film had just been made. Entitled *Ferry to Hong Kong*, it told the story of a stateless person who was ill-advised enough to board this little ship in Hong Kong, just as I had done. The authorities refused to let him enter Macao and, when the ferry returned to Hong Kong, the people there did the same. So he went backwards and forwards between them for nearly a year before a South American country took pity on him and accepted him.

It seemed only a matter of time before China grabbed both these foreign enclaves on her mainland. Anti-Red China feeling was strong in Macao, but already the flag of China flew alongside that of Portugal on the streets. A causeway to China was being built and I saw men working on it at gunpoint. I was stopped one hundred yards from the ornate stone gateway at the frontier and warned not to take photographs. I did sneak one, and at the sound of the camera shutter, my trishaw driver drew his finger across his throat. He took me on an interesting tour, passing the house of Sun Yat Sen, the founder of modern China. He had graduated in medicine at Hong Kong and became president of China in 1911 after getting rid of the Manchus. We also drove part of the way past the pits of the Macao Grand Prix, and I bought joss sticks at an old Chinese temple. Many Portuguese troops were in the streets, including men from one of their African regiments. Some houses are in the Portuguese style, with red and green wooden shutters and gardens full of flowers. I stayed at the Bela Vista hotel, home to visiting Europeans. This had clean, bare rooms with odd little baths attached, and a smell of garlic pervading all. The town was centred on the Casino, where the Chinese gamble throughout the twenty-four hours. The main game is Fan Tan, an ancient and simple way of betting on whether one, two, three or four counters will be left when a random pile is removed by the croupier, four at a time. To accommodate the numbers wishing to play, holes are cut in the floor above each table, with railings round them. Bets are lowered to the tables below in little baskets.

The Ecolegia de Santa Rosa de Lima was interesting and a little scary. It was such a beautiful building that I wished to see more of it. I received permission from someone on the gate to see the grounds, but too late realised I was walking around a nunnery. Many of the nuns were Chinese. Escape was quickly cut off, as they were holding a fete for charity that afternoon, and insisted on showing me what they had done for it. All Macao, they said, would be attending. I eventually arrived at the main church in the college grounds, the interior of which was pure white and very beautiful. It was absolutely silent and I thought it was empty, until I realised that the all-white figure, kneeling in front of the altar, was a nun at prayer. At this point, I really felt that I was in the wrong place, and fled.

Having done my tourist bit in Macao, I returned on the ferry to Hong Kong and the Navy.

14

To the South Seas: Manus and Fiji

Now all my thoughts were on the forthcoming cruise to the South Pacific. Fortunately the Quemoy/Formosa situation did not alter, and thus the anticipated cruise could proceed unchallenged. The annual Fleet Regatta was behind us, and my sole contribution had been to examine the boxers before their fights and to be on hand during the bouts. I then joined *Crane* for the trip south.

Just before we left the surgeon captain in Singapore wrote me a letter asking if I would sign-on for a short-service commission. This was tempting, as I had just realised that I would be coming to the end of my national service when *Crane* returned to Singapore. I had, as yet, no clear idea of what kind of medical career I wished to follow, and the fun I had in the Royal Navy had led to little thought for the future. I had enjoyed an excellent time travel-wise, with more to come, but I had to remember the unfortunates who had spent all their time in relatively boring shore jobs. Medically the frigates had provided some excitements, along with the expected amount of routine. A short-term attraction, being put about, was a trip to Phnom Penh in Cambodia, but I decided not to take up the surgeon captain's offer, at least in the meantime.

So we left Hong Kong, in my case, probably for the final time. On the journey south the sea was really rough, as we edged our way along the outskirts of typhoon 'Nancy' which was centred near Guam. This meant that we travelled down the west coast of the Philippines, rather than the east as we did last time. We had good views of the coastline of some of the islands, especially Luzon, Mindoro and Mindanao. All were mountainous and covered in trees, with palms along the edges of sandy beaches and little sign of habitation.

We passed once more through the Basilan Strait and turned east along the fifth parallel of latitude until, nine days out from Singapore, we finally headed south to cross the Equator. 'Crossing the line' caused great hilarity, with a heavily disguised Father Neptune climbing aboard over the starboard bow. Novices, or 'first timers', were unceremoniously 'shaved' with a gigantic brush and razor and tipped backward, a la Sweeney Todd, into a canvas bath of sea water. The captain was the first to be ducked.

After ten days at sea in rough conditions, the thought of a stable bunk to sleep on became quite attractive. The following letter gives some idea of what it can be like to cross an open ocean in a small ship:

In spite of the loud creaking of the ship, the occasional crash of breaking crockery and the breaking loose of the heavy wardroom table during lunch the other day, we are listening to the Test Match commentary. We are doing well. The table incident was quite funny. I had finished lunch and was sitting with others on a long bench which runs along the starboard side of the wardroom. The wardroom measures about eighteen feet square. We were facing inboard, and were laughing at the navigating officer who had arrived late and was facing us. We were amused at the pained expression on his face as he held his soup plate clear of the table. We quickly stopped laughing, however, when at the apex of a particularly heavy roll, the table broke away and slid down towards us. I remember pulling my legs up quickly and getting ready to jump. I also remember the navigator sitting on his tethered chair with no table in front of him, his soup plate in his left hand and his spoon in the right. Unfortunately, what goes up must come down, and he departed rapidly when the table turned back towards him. Gerard Hoffnung's story of the barrel of bricks came to mind. The table was caught before too much damage was done, and doubly lashed back in position. That's what happens when you are only 1,500 tons.

Our first port of call was Manus, also known as Great Admiralty Island, largest of the Admiralty Islands. They lie two hundred miles north of the island of New Guinea. We only had twenty-four hours at Manus, but what a twenty-four hours it was. This is a small island, part of the New Guinea group, which means it was still very primitive. Fifty whites ran the Royal Australian Navy refuelling base and there is an indigenous Melanesian population of fifteen hundred. The defence of the Naval base was in the hands of the PIR or Pacific Islands Regiment. This small regiment was made up of terrifying, locally-entered troops under Australian officers. Little, it seemed, would be stolen from that base.

The Australian navy's doctor, a Scot called McGregor, quickly came on board. He had coffee and then went to the ship's shop where he bought sweets and models for his four girls, aged four to eleven, who were with him and his wife on the island. We went ashore and he took me to his hospital, which was very clean, modem and well equipped but had no patients. He was from Edinburgh but found life as a GP in Scotland too dull and was now on a four-year commission with the Australian navy. The only help he had on the island were a Navy dentist and an Australian nurse. His stories of the island were hair-raising. One night, going in to see if his youngest daughter was asleep, he found a snake coiled on her bedpost.

At lunchtime there was an RPC in HMAS *Tauranga*, the Australian naval base. This was another 'stone frigate', although 'wood and thatch' was probably more accurate than 'stone'. 'RPC' was the usual naval shorthand for 'Request Pleasure of your Company', the answers being 'WMP' or 'MRU', which stand for 'with much pleasure', and 'much regret unable'. After lunch I was lucky enough to visit a native village, the only man from the ship to do so. This was fascinating and, as will be seen, was possible only because I had met McGregor. It was interesting to see that even he ventured into this village with a little trepidation, although he took his daughters with us. 'Take this strong stick,' he said, 'and leave your camera in the Land Rover; they think it's the evil eye or something.' What good the strong stick would do I could not see. We first went along a rough track through steamy mangrove swamps where he shot crocodiles, some of them fifteen feet in length. Many snakes lived in these swamps. Approaching the village he parked the Land Rover and we walked the rest of the way.

The village had an idyllic setting, located as it was on a narrow stretch of golden sand beneath palm trees, with outrigger canoes pulled up onto the beach. The canoes were very simple, consisting of only hollowed-out palm trunks supported by an outrigger on one side. There were only a few houses, arranged in a semicircle around a central clearing. The houses were on stilts, or on pillars made from oil drums. The living area was approximately nine feet above ground-level and reached by a rough ladder with a few, irregular rungs. Roofs were of coconut thatch, here and there supplemented by ex-wartime corrugated iron. This area was American, their invasion of the Philippines being partly launched from here. As we walked in, we passed the 'bachelors' hut, a ground-level structure which we thought would be an insult to hens.

The Polynesian people of the eastern Pacific are as strikingly good looking as Captain Bligh found to his cost on Tahiti. Not so the Melanesians. McGregor told me that their neighbours on the next island still engaged in a little cannibalism and that the parents of those we were visiting had also eaten human flesh. I did begin to wonder if he was exaggerating in some of his story telling, but the appearance of the young men of the village quickly dispelled this thought. They followed us around in silence, unsmiling. McGregor handed out smarties to the native children who accompanied us, some of these sugar-coated sweets being shyly offered by his own daughters. His youngest, Isla, became very upset about this, as she saw all her sweets disappearing. There was, however, an ominous feeling in the air.

The people were almost completely naked, very black except where painted with grey clay, and, by our standards, not beautiful. The few half-Japanese among them – a legacy of the war – were, it has to be said, very ugly. One old woman sat cross-legged on the platform of her house looking down at us, silent and unsmiling. Through her nasal septum was a six-inch bone and she was short of many teeth. Those she had left were stained bright red with the betel nut she chewed. She was heavily tattooed and her ears showed the disfiguration seen on many of the old women. The rim of the ear is detached all the way round except at the front. The rim is then left to shrivel and form a bizarre type of earring.

The headman of the village appeared. He was a small elderly figure, almost naked like the others, but appeared dignified and very solemn. McGregor spoke to him in Melanesian pidgin, telling him who I was. 'All same fella doctor blong ship,' he said, but only when he had reassured the old man that I was definitely leaving the following day was there any sign of relaxation. Then I had my hand shaken for a very long time while he looked me straight in the face and confirmed repeatedly that I was leaving the next day.

McGregor was undoubtedly accepted in the village. He said that he alone amongst the white population of Manus could walk here because he had occasionally looked after them. As proof, he brought forward a young woman and her baby. He asked her to show me her ankles. She had short scars, the site of 'cut down' drips. The story told was a good one. The woman had nearly died in labour. Her people, against the wishes of some, carried her through the bush to the small Navy hospital. She was near the point of death and McGregor had great difficulty in getting a drip up. This was the reason for the drip sites on her ankles, an extreme measure. She recovered and produced a healthy baby. The doctor asked her to tell me the baby's name. 'McGregor!' she said and laughed. This was the first time I had heard laughter in the village, and it was a happy note on which to leave.

The expats threw a great party for us in the evening, after which I decided that I would see the Australian nurse back to her bungalow. The transport dropped us off, but this meant I had left myself with no means of returning to the ship. I therefore had to walk in the dark on a jungle path. I made it just before sailing time, and gave the gangway sentry a fright as I appeared out of the darkness. He had thought that everyone was aboard. Looking back on it, I realised how stupid I had been to walk that path in darkness, despite the fact that I arrived at the ship unscathed. The nocturnal wildlife of Manus was not to be taken lightly.

The seamen's mess deck awarded me the 'Manus Medal' after this episode, one of only two struck. The other went to the 'chippie'. Then we sailed for Fiji.

We left Manus at the break of a tropical dawn. The captain of *Crane* decided that he would like to have a look at other places on the way to Fiji, which suited me very well. Rabaul is the only town in New Britain, another of New Guinea's many islands. The harbour there is a flooded caldera, surrounded by intermittently active volcanoes. The whole region is volcanically unstable, which means that the harbour may have changed in the last few months. We passed a smoking volcano on the starboard side on the way in, had a quick look at Rabaul, and left. The small columns of smoke all around were not volcanic, but from open air cooking fires. Rabaul was more developed than Manus – it would be impossible not to be – which was why the Australian nurse was to come to the island shortly to restock with clothes after she had lost some in a fire.

Guadalcanal is famous for the fighting between the Americans and the Japanese that took place on the island during World War II. Wrecked landing craft were still lying on the beaches. We went down 'The Slot', the channel that divides the Solomon Islands into two groups, and crossed the bay in which the Japanese lost several cruisers. Off Malaita, one of the Solomons, we had arranged a meeting with the survey ship HMSS *Cook*. The object of this was to hand over her cat. It had been on a run ashore when they left Hong Kong some considerable time ago, but almost unbelievably, one of our sailors recognised it in the street. Knowing that *Cook* was surveying in this area, he brought it down for them.

Our arrival at Fiji was tremendous. The harbour of Suva, the capital, is beautiful. It sits in a large lagoon inside the reef. The water is turquoise and sparkles in the sun. They had turned out the police band to play us alongside, and a splendid sight the bandsmen were too. They were all over six feet, wearing navy blue and scarlet tunics and white 'sulus'. These are scallop-hemmed long skirts, common attire for Fijian men. Their bare legs are shod with huge open leather sandals. Their hair added a good six inches to their height, being allowed to grow thick and bushy. Fijian women are also large and fat. A photograph of our navigating officer, who is short and thin, trying to reach round one of these ladies to embrace her for the camera, was very funny. He looked to be in danger of severe injury by crushing. The difference between these large women and the *cheong-sam* wearing ladies of Hong Kong was a world apart. At a neighbouring jetty a ship was just leaving for Tonga, and her send-off was an occasion for much merriment and music.

Half the population of Fiji is now Indian, which leads to racial tension. One Indian, a cassava farmer, having heard that we were thinking of hiring

Fiji. Policeman on points duty, wearing a 'sulu'

a car, said, 'Be careful. Don't stop in villages. Too much thumping the man.' The Indians run many of the shops, some of them protecting their goods by metal grilles. This friction was a pity as the native Fijians seemed a happy people and unaware, until too late, of the Indian take-over of their island. I was puzzled by a sign on a fish stall in the open market, which read 'Today's Poisonous Fish'. Were they for sale? Two ships were in harbour loading copra and sugar for the UK.

We spent some time at Laucala Bay as guests of the RNZAF and the Fiji Armed Forces. The highlight there was a boat trip out to the reef. It was too rough for my feeble swimming and I contented myself with climbing down the mooring rope to see the coral. The New Zealanders shot two blue angels with a harpoon gun. These are skate-sized and said to be good eating. A turtle swimming past caused great excitement, but the undertow was too strong for even the scuba divers to get away from the side of the boat.

Before we left for our next, very unusual port of call, the Fijians had laid on two visits for us. The first was to Tamavua, a native 'show' village with palm thatch as in the old days. The second was to the Legislative Assembly in Suva. This was an impressive place, open to the air as much as possible and very quiet. The members of the Assembly were three Fijians, three Indians and three whites. One of the latter, on hearing that we were New Zealand bound, told me that his daughter had been Fiji's 'Miss Hibiscus'. She was now living in Wellington and he suggested that I should contact her. That seemed a very good idea.

15

The Kermadec Islands and New Zealand

The original plan was that the ship would go directly from Suva to Auckland, but this was changed at the request of the New Zealand Civil Aviation Authority. The Kermadec Islands lie in the box on the International Date Line, which means that they share the same day of the week as countries that lie to the west of them. As the islands are uninhabited, one wonders why it was thought necessary so to bend the hundred and eighty degree line of longitude, but I had long been fascinated by this anomaly and was glad that we were now Kermadec bound. We were to call at one of them, Sunday Island or Raoul. Now we could say, quite literally, that we had been on the other side of the world.

The New Zealand authorities maintained a weather station on this island, with ten men spending a year there and being visited by their supply ship once every six months. There was no airstrip on the island and it was far from helicopter range of land. One of the weathermen had developed what sounded like a pilonidal abscess and we were asked to assess whether he needed repatriation, or just an antibiotic. I was to go ashore and decide. A relief weatherman was sent up to Fiji, to come with us on the journey south. As Christmas was upon us, he was naturally reluctant to spend it in this lonely place. 'I'm sure some tablets will do him, Doc,' he said, and I promised to oblige him if I could.

*Kermadec Islands. Sunday Island or Raoul. The island is completely
surrounded by cliffs meaning that there is no landing place*

To reach the Kermadecs meant a detour of nearly three hundred miles to
the southeast. We arrived off Sunday Island on a beautiful Sunday morning,
but at once there was a problem. The captain had suspected that he might
have difficulty getting the ship in close and, when he had seen the situation
for himself, he realised the correctness of this judgement . He felt he had to
remain a good distance offshore because of the poorly surveyed seabed around
the island, and because there were known to be difficult currents. He pulled
a face as he looked at the chart and then, brightening up, said, 'It's a beautiful
morning, Doc, I'm going to send the sea boat in instead of the motorboat. It's
time they had something to do.'

The Cornish bosun's mate piped 'Away sea boat's ca-rew' and there was
a rushing of feet as the boat was launched. At the start of the commission the
sea boat's crew had been nominated, but they had had few chances to man
their boat: normally the motorboat was used. From my point of view, just

as for the seamen, who thoroughly enjoyed their change from routine, the choice could not have been better. Although embarrassing to admit, I was aware of the romance and history of the situation. The idea of travelling in a small boat under oar to a remote island in poorly surveyed seas, was like a throwback to bygone days. The only sound I heard as I sat in the stern was the splashing of the oars. I doubt, however, if the met man agreed, as he weighed his chances of spending Christmas so far from home.

It became more obvious as we approached the cliff-bound island that there was no obvious landing place. At no point could a boat even be beached. How I was to get ashore nobody in the boat had clue, and so it remained, until we arrived right under the cliffs. Then, looking up, I saw what looked like a small laundry basket being lowered on a wire rope. The boat was manoeuvred to lie briefly alongside the basket and I jumped in, holding on to the wire. Unfortunately – and here Hoffnung's hilarious story of the basket of bricks flashed through my mind for the second time since leaving Hong Kong – the winch man on the cliff top had lowered the basket just too far. The stretching of the wicker basket, combined with the stretching of the cable and my weight, meant that the basket and I disappeared beneath the surface. This was greeted with loud laughter from the boat but happily the winch operator spotted his error, and the basket and I were rapidly recovered and quickly hauled up.

All the men on the island had come to the winch point and, while the boss man had brought a detailed medical history with him, one look at the suffering meteorologist was enough. He had a large abscess and a spreading cellulitis. He therefore required repatriation, and the news was shouted down to his colleague in the boat. I heard later that his language when he heard this news shocked even *Crane's* sailors. Just to rub it in, one of the men up top shouted down that the newcomer was due to be on call that night. The victim apart, the men all looked very fit as a result of their open-air existence. The island, they said, had deer, wild pig and many rats.

The abscess went down first, and when the basket came up again it contained a gift of beer and cigarettes from *Crane's* ship's company who had had a whip-round. I had only time for a short conversation, and then the basket was winched out and I returned to the boat. Finally the relief weatherman was hauled up, and we returned through spray to the ship. *Crane* looked very impressive from wave top height and I enjoyed a big Sunday lunch. I felt very pleased that I had become one of the few people to set foot on this island.

Later I read that the sea around Sunday Island was one of the few authenticated places where giant squid have been spotted. We did not meet one, but some Japanese fishermen had recently and the experience had terrified them. Norwegian waters are said to be the home of the fictional Kraken. This South Seas equivalent, however, is only too real. Three days later we arrived in Auckland in time for Christmas.

Christmas Day was great fun. Captain's Rounds were held as usual but with the difference that the youngest man on the ship, a seventeen year old, was dressed in the captain's uniform and acted his part. The captain brought up the rear of the inspecting party wearing a sailor's hat. The mess decks were decorated with streamers, and nuts were laid out in patterns on mess tables. 'Tot time' or rum issue occurred during rounds, and it was then that one found out who one's true friends were. As has been mentioned before, rum and its disposal are taken seriously in the Navy. I learned this the hard way, being faced with a long series of 'Sippers, sir!' or 'Gulpers, sir!' This means that one is being offered either a sip or a gulp of a man's tot. To refuse it is very bad form, but when it comes to 'See it off, sir!' one is in trouble. This is an invitation to drink half a man's tot, the biggest amount allowed, and this has to be downed in one swallow. A spontaneous concert, not of carols, then began in the forward seaman's mess deck, from which I could not get away even when officers were piped to muster in the wardroom for Christmas lunch. Eventually we sat down to lunch three short, they being in their bunks. Another, a sub-lieutenant, quietly folded up during the meal. The remaining eight of us had a good Christmas meal, with turkey replaced by chicken. It was then decided that each of us should make a speech. This ended up being hilarious, made more so by the now immense affability of the listeners, rather than the wit of the speakers. For example, I included a joke which I thought was only slightly funny. To my amazement the rest were reduced to prolonged and helpless mirth, some banging the table. I had told this joke once before at a student nurses' dinner. It had gone down well there, but nothing to equal this.

After lunch I went swimming with one of the hospital nurses whom I had met very early in the day, when I went up to Auckland hospital with a rating who had reported sick. The poor man had chosen that day to have a haemoptysis, fortunately later found to be from cystic bronchiectasis and, therefore, not infectious. The girl had a car, which was just as well, as the beach and the sea were not warm.

Auckland was a dull place. It reminded me of Inverness but with one main street and no soul. The houses were mostly wooden with verandas and what, in an American Western, would be a hitching rail. There seemed to be many small men in large hats with turned-in toes, and many of the women wore sack dresses. Noel Coward was right when he said that he 'went to New Zealand last Wednesday but it was closed!' Certainly many people were away for the Christmas holiday, and all the way round New Zealand we saw that weekends spent in the countryside were much enjoyed. Many people had cabins by the lakes and were much involved in all sorts of country pursuits. Hydrangeas grow wild in large numbers, much as daffodils do in Scotland.

From Auckland we headed to Tauranga, a holiday resort, to give sea-cadets some sea time. A visit to Rotorua gave us a sight of boiling mud, geysers and Maoris, and then it was back to Auckland and eventually the port of Lyttleton. This is Christchurch's port, a town with some attractive buildings, and kindly but dire invitations to the ship's company. The sailors were invited back to people's houses for Christmas parties, only to find on arrival that these consisted of singing carols around pianos.

Things came alive at last in Timaru. Here the wardroom gave another cocktail party and I met the daughter of one of the local sheep farmers here on the Canterbury Plain. She asked if I and any others would like to go with her and her father for a day's wallaby shooting. Four of us went and it turned out to be a fantastic day. The owner of the farm, which covers seven thousand acres, was a retired doctor turned sheep farmer. He and his wife were pretty old and the farm was really run by their two daughters. It was situated thirty miles from Timaru, and we shot over the hillside where the mountains run down to the plain. This was the only region in New Zealand where wallabies are found. They were introduced from Australia as an experiment to harvest them for their fur, but had become a pest, eating young grass and trees. They look like small grey kangaroos and their gait makes them difficult to hit.

We covered many miles on foot, often through bush scrub, ascending to three thousand feet. The total shot was ten, of which I got one. I also escaped a 303 bullet fired by a sub-lieutenant, very close to my left ear, after which I had a word in both of his. We were out from nine in the morning until eight in the evening and then returned to the farmhouse where a fantastic meal was waiting.

We ate thick vegetable soup, huge platefuls of Canterbury lamb and new potatoes, and finished with raspberries and ice cream. There was unlimited home-brewed cider and New Zealand beer. It was difficult to hold ourselves back on the lamb and they were very keen to keep us eating. Some of the girls we had met on the ship had been invited out from Timaru and we had a great time, getting back to the ship around dawn. This day was a huge success, making up for a rather disappointing cruise so far. The sailors had had a mixed day. They apparently were very smart as they marched through the town as part of its Centennial celebrations, but the dance laid on for them came to an abrupt end when buses arrived to take the girls home at midnight.

The Scottish Free Church founded Dunedin, the next and most southerly port of call for *Crane*. There are still many Scottish names in the town, including Canongate, Corstorphine and St Kilda. Inevitably, after Timaru, it was a rather dull place. Wellington, New Zealand's capital, also seemed like just another town.

I quickly tracked down Fiji's 'Miss Hibiscus' and lost no time in getting her down to the ship where she wowed everybody. Unfortunately, I stood rather heavily on her foot while dancing in my less-than-perfect style. The wardroom carpet did not help. Next day we went to the Wellington Racing Club's summer meeting at Trentham.

Before leaving for Australia we took Wellington sea cadets to Picton. This picturesque place is tucked away in a maze of channels, in the north-west corner of the country's South Island. It was so hidden that the navigator missed it on his first attempt to find the right channel. The first we knew about it was when the ship turned one hundred and eighty degrees and the Captain made the sardonic pipe, 'D'ye hear there? Will anyone knowing the way in to Picton please contact the navigating officer.' Thus much laughter was had at that officer's expense.

New Zealand, with one or two notable exceptions such as the wallaby shoot, had been a disappointment. Perhaps it was too like a staid Victorian version of home, or perhaps we had just spent too long in more exotic places, but 'dull' was the word we all used for the place. As we headed further north to the much livelier Australia, the albatrosses that had accompanied us around the coast, now left us, and returned to their home waters.

16

Australia and through Indonesian waters

Our time in Australia was short and our port of call only one: Cairns in north Queensland. The Tasman Sea produced a steady roll and took a week to cross, travelling, as we did, to the northwest. We came inside the Great Barrier Reef well to the south and anchored for a short time at Magnetic Island, to allow people to swim behind shark nets. Albatrosses abandoned us as the temperature rose, and it was a surprise to find out that Cairns is situated well into the tropics. It was also a surprise to find that this small town is approximately one thousand miles from the state capital, Brisbane. Sugar exporting seemed to be its main industry.

In spite of its seeming isolation, Cairns was as different as could be from any New Zealand town we had visited. The houses had their living areas on the first floor, as in Manus, presumably for coolness. The variety of brightly coloured flowers was striking. More striking still was the remarkable difference in the people. Where the New Zealanders were worthy, quiet and quite happy and while in Wellington it was not possible to buy a drink after half past seven in the evening, the Australians were very much alive: "Oh! You've come from New Zealand' they said at the reception given for us on arrival, 'we're going to take it over next week!' This summed up the difference between the countries as I saw it. The welcoming reception should have finished in the early evening but went on until nearly midnight. We encountered nothing like this in New Zealand.

At various receptions, including one given by the Far North Queensland Regiment, the people all made a point of telling us how much room there was for us if we cared to emigrate. We met many interesting people. The pathologist and his wife gave me supper. A padre had a parish the size of England and Wales, and we met a Latvian who was on a single-handed small boat trip round the world. They had laid on a superb programme of visits for us. The Flying Doctor service allowed us to listen in to calls from all over north Queensland, some medical, many not so. One man wanted spare parts for a tractor, and, another, two big Australian-type bush hats. Their aircraft included a Cessna and an Auster, several of the latter also belonging to Bush Pilots Limited, a charter firm. At a small zoo, along with wallabies, kangaroos and crocodiles, our interest was centred on a taipan, – a large venomous snake, which was housed in a decidedly rickety cage without a lock.

A local dentist took two of us on a drive around the tableland, which lies high up behind Cairns. There are over two hundred varieties of bird in this area. The land is given over to sugar cane plantations, monkey-nut growing and eucalyptus trees, called 'gums' in these parts. A massive hydroelectric plant was being built near the aboriginal town of Waipa in the far north. Impressive and quite strange to us, were the termite, or white ant 'hills'. These stood six to seven feet high among the gums. Deposits of bauxite have been found here in quantity and add to the general feeling of prosperity.

There was no doubt about how lively this country was, compared with the much more inhibited New Zealand. It was difficult to leave, but at least we had the anticipation of returning to Singapore via Indonesian waters although we did not call anywhere en route.

We left Cairns at the north end of the Great Barrier Reef and travelled briefly through the Pacific before entering the Coral Sea. Then we headed into the Torres Strait, rounding Cape York, the most northerly point of Australia, named in 1770 by Captain Cook. It was here, close to the Cape on a calm evening, that we saw the finest sunset that I ever expect to see. Standing on the open bridge, I looked in silence with those on watch. The sky was a mass of reds, blues and greens, outlining the western horizon. It was so still that the flying fish were travelling in straight lines over the flat sea. Normally they use even the slightest ripple to zig-zag, giving them some degree of concealment.

The Arafura Sea, with the Torres Strait, is notoriously dangerous to shipping because of the many poorly charted reefs. We entered Indonesian waters where the Arafura and the Banda seas meet, and then carried on into the Flores Sea. The islands of Flores and Timor were steep-to and heavily wooded. We only saw one house on Flores. It was red-roofed and set in a clearing high on a mountain, looking as if it could fall into the sea at any moment. I remember thinking that the woodcutter might be rather lonely, but at least he had a view second to none.

If the sunset off Cape York was the finest I expect to see, the storm that hit *Crane* shortly after passing Flores was the worst I ever expect to endure. It arrived suddenly, from nowhere. The sky darkened to black and sheet lightening lit everything up. The upper deck rapidly became unsafe, in spite of the safety wire strung along it, and I went up to the bridge via the internal ladder. The sight was impressive. The sea had suddenly become a dirty yellow-white, with a screaming gale which roared through the rigging. Huge breaking waves led to spray and foam being picked up by the gale and flung higher than *Crane's* open bridge. Wind and current were in opposition, which meant that the waves had become confused and lumpy, with no order to them. Caught in this, the ship plunged about, trying hard to maintain steerage-way. Overhead the black clouds were low, producing a feeling of being trapped in an awful, enclosed world. At one point a water spout formed, a sort of pillar of water connecting the sea with the clouds. Sheets of water quickly soaked all those on the bridge and waves washed right over the quarterdeck. I went to see how the cooks were coping with the violent motion, but need not have worried. Everything in the galley was as normal, the only exception being that the pots on the stove were lashed down. The storm lasted for an hour or so and produced remarkably little damage.

The final part of the journey was through the South China Sea and then the Johore Strait. This was to be the last time that I went through this beautiful stretch of water.

17

Singapore, Suez and Portsmouth

It was almost time for me to return to the UK, having completed the time laid down for a national serviceman. Meantime I moved back into the country house atmosphere of *Terror*'s officer mess, and enjoyed the comfort and the good food. Each morning I cycled down to the dockyard on one of the Navy's bicycles. These were painted white to prevent theft, and I thoroughly enjoyed this means of transport, especially in the relatively cool early morning. I had not cycled since my school days. My relief arrived, also from Edinburgh, and I handed over to him. He looked slightly bemused, as probably I had done in his place, but at least he would not have the antiquated stores to sort out.

I was now free to negotiate my trip back to Britain. Normally this was by air, and some of my contemporaries had already taken the plane. I wanted to see Suez and the Mediterranean, however, and I knew it was occasionally possible to go home by sea. I went to see the fleet movements officer, who made all the decisions. He was helpful. 'Well,' he said, 'these troopships are usually for accompanied service personnel … unless of course … ', and here he paused and laid one finger on the side of his nose, 'unless you had a medical reason for NOT going by air?' Very quickly I remembered a bout of Singapore Ear (*otitis externa*) I had contracted some months before. 'That would do,' he said, 'I think I can swing it.' It took a few days arrange and I then

128

heard from him that he had booked me on the next sailing of the *Oxfordshire*, leaving the main commercial harbour of Singapore in one month's time. He winked as I collected my ticket.

Now I had absolutely nothing to do and it was this inactivity that nearly landed me in serious trouble. A sub-lieutenant (SD), that is a man commissioned from the lower deck at an older age, suggested to myself and another lieutenant that we visit Amy's Bar in Johore Bahru. This was in Malaya and was strictly off-limits to naval personnel, as was everywhere across the causeway. It had become well known to British residents of Malaya, and of Singapore, for no particular reason that I could see, but being across the causeway it was definitely not for us. Had I known the reputation of this sub-lieutenant for aggression when in his cups, I would not have gone, but neither I nor the third man present knew him. So, being bored, and feeling that this would be quite an exciting way to finish a great stay in the Far East, I shared a taxi and crossed over into Malaya. Amy's turned out to be the simplest of small clean bars, with only a handful of people in it, drinking Tiger beer. It seemed a bit of a frost but after one or two pints the situation changed rapidly – and for the worse.

We had been talking to some of the Malayans. One of them said something which I did not hear, but 'X' did. The first I knew that we were in trouble was his bellow of anger. He leapt to his feet and seized the small Malayan, with the obvious intention of inflicting further damage. To do so, as a commissioned officer in the Navy, was a court martial offence, and we were, of course, already breaking rules by being in an out-of-bounds country. Prompt action was called for. The other guy and I also leapt to our feet, and tried to haul him off. This was no easy task as he was a large man, but by dint of kicking him behind the knees we diverted his anger on to us. This was at least better, and we kept him off his victim until a taxi arrived. We made it back to Singapore and no more was heard of it. The SD lieutenant was not pleased, but the third man and I were relieved. It was interesting to speculate on what the powers-that-be would have done if he had really assaulted the guy.

There was a semi-organised farewell party in *Terror's* officers' club the night before *Oxfordshire* sailed. The highlight was the round after round of sausages with tomato ketchup, washed down with the famous Tiger beer. The little Chinese steward fell asleep on his stool between rounds, as we played ten-pin bowling with a steady decrease in skill. The evening finished eventually, amid much merriment, at half past five in the morning. I had then to pack the rest of my belongings, and cross Singapore Island in a rush to catch the ship which sailed at an early hour. And so it was that I left the Far East.

While I would see Suez and the Med, the troopship was heavy going compared to the liveliness of the frigates. I shared a table at meal times with the medics on the ship's staff and found them all rather solemn. There was a moment of sheer terror when I discovered from the ship's notice board that I was down to organise the children's sports. I considered this and happily I realised that this horrific event must happen on every sailing, and I sought out the *Oxfordshire*'s bos'un. As anticipated, he had laid out the nets and other equiptment each time, and had seen many sports days. I organised a compliant nursing sister from the ship's sick quarters to help him and spent the day skulking in the background. The occasion passed without a hitch.

Our first port of call was Colombo, an interesting town of many contrasts. There was enough time to see the main part of the town, and to be glad that we did not live there. Bullock carts mingled with Mercedes in the main street. A crowd of children had gathered outside a souvenir shop, giggling and saying 'Orson Welles! ... oh! yes! ... Orson Welles! It is, it is!' The door of the shop opened, and a large man with a cigar rushed out to a car waiting for him. 'I've got to have ten dollars, I mean rupees' he shouted, at whoever was in the car, and then he rushed back into the shop, ignoring the girls.

The next call was at Aden, where I called at *Sheba*, handed over some tickets I still had for the Gold Mohur swimming club, and chatted with one or two people still in this godforsaken place. It was most definitely a place to leave as fast as possible. Then we travelled around the corner and up to the Red Sea and the Suez Canal. We arrived in Suez Bay at 3pm. and anchored there until 8am the following day, when the sixteen ships that made up the next north-bound convoy had gathered. Then we had a further wait in the Bitter Lakes, halfway up the eighty-nine mile length, until the first southbound convoy of the day had cleared the upper part of the canal. The second southbound convoy was tied up in a 'lay by' between the Lakes and Port Said as we passed. This staggering of convoys means each passes through the one-way canal more quickly. It took fourteen hours to go from Suez to Port Said. On the starboard side there was nothing to see but desert and camels until Sinai, where Mig jets were flying around. They were also flying low over the airfield at Ismailia, with a dozen others on the ground, each in its blast proof shelter. On the port side of the canal, people in flowing robes rode mules bareback, sometimes at speed, and looked quite Biblical. A 'gully gully' man joined the ship at Suez and left at Port Said. These men are peculiar to the Suez Canal and are freelance conjurers. The Canal was well worth the decision to opt for a sea journey home, but it proved to be downhill all the way thereafter.

At Limassol in Cyprus, we embarked some soldiery from a series of launches, which meant that we only got as far as the harbour entrance. The town looked attractive with its red roofs, cream walls and minarets, set against tall mountains. It was a surprise to see snow on the mountains of Crete and we passed Cape Bon in North Africa, site of the German surrender in World War II. Gibraltar is unbelievably dull in spite of its romantic history. It appeared to consist of narrow streets, small shops and bullfight advertisements. We trooped ashore in miserably wet weather and it was clear that the holiday was over.

Thirty-six hours later we passed Cape Finisterre and the Bay of Biscay. Off Lisbon the sardine boats were busy. Finally, we arrived at Portsmouth.

18

The Shetland Isles

While I was pleased to be back home, I felt restless. I knew I had to decide between remaining in the Navy, which I had the opportunity of doing, and returning to civilian life. I could see the advantages of both but I realised that a naval career could not always be expected to be as exciting and interesting as mine had been so far. I applied for a job with the British Antarctic Survey but was turned down on the grounds, so they said, that I 'was too young and too inexperienced'. I was inclined to disagree, but they may have been right. In the meantime, I saw an advertisement in the BMA office in Edinburgh for a locum to cover a change of doctor on the island of Unst in the Shetlands. This was the most northerly Shetland Island and therefore the most northerly practice in Britain. It sounded interesting. I applied and was successful. The decision I had to make about careers could now be put off again, this time for six weeks.

So I headed to Shetland, flying from Aberdeen and then travelling by 'special hire'. This meant a taxi from Sumburgh to Lerwick, and then onwards to the north end of the Shetland mainland. Then I took a ferry crossing to Yell, a taxi up the length of this island, another ferry over to Unst and there, on the jetty, was the island's district nurse. 'Oh!', she said, in a surprised but not hostile voice, 'a young doctor!' She had come down the eight miles from the main village on the island to meet me and to show me around.

I was to stay with the unmarried son and daughter of a long dead doctor who, many years before, had written a definitive book on the birds of Unst. The doctor who had just left the island had gone to a practice on the Shetland mainland, and apart from his surgery, his house was empty. I walked through the empty rooms, hearing the wind, always present in Shetland, whistling around the house. Through the windows one could see only barren hills and moor. I found these conditions stimulating, and right away the decision that I had to make began to form. I had come here of my own choice and, for six weeks, the health of the thousand people on the island were in my hands. After that, the next move was again to be up to me, not someone else, and this freedom had a lot to be said for it.

The next six weeks were just what I wished for. This island was new to me and I had the previous doctor's Land Rover with which to explore it. There were many birds, good fishing and magnificent coastal scenery. I had simple but adequate accommodation and a large supply of good food. Things were definitely looking up.

From a medical perspective, many events stood out, but probably the one of which I was the most proud happened late at night, when a gale was blowing. The patient was an old lady who lived in the most northerly house on Unst. She was therefore the most northerly person in Great Britain and, by definition, the most northerly patient of the National Health Service. I set off in the Land Rover, drove the ten miles up to the north end of the island, and on the way picked up the sister who had phoned me. She was walking back to the house from a public call box. The old lady had what I called a 'stuck' inguinal hernia. Was it reducible, or was it strangulated? If the latter, urgent surgery was required. This was an example of the risks of living on a remote island, the nearest surgeon being located in Lerwick on the Shetland mainland. The old woman would have to reverse the journey I had made, which would involve three ambulances and two ferries. This on a stormy night, and when she was in considerable pain, was not desirable. I tried gently to reduce the hernia, acutely aware of the risk of rupturing it. I thought it did retreat back somewhat, but it seemed incomplete. Her pain, however, was lessened. I decided to await events and made a probably useless splint from a broad Elastoplast tin, bandages and cotton wool.

Muckle Flugga lighthouse, Shetland. This lighthouse is on a small steep islet, the most northerly point of the Shetland Islands and therefore of Great Britain

Her sister helped raise the foot of the bed on volumes of the Encyclopaedia Britannica. Next morning I was relieved to find her much better, and she was eventually seen in a less dramatic fashion as a surgical outpatient.

Another event caused me surprise in a community of hardy people. The common cold, it seemed, had to be treated. The patient was an old man, very much ex-Service. Reassurance that he had a self-limiting illness for which no medicine was necessary was treated with contempt. This was a dispensing practice, which meant that all medicines were purchased and handed out by the doctor. Faced with this situation, I looked in the medicine cupboard, found a bottle of a harmless green proprietary 'cough mixture', and dispensed a small quantity. It was, of course, no good, but the man came back, asking for something else. Advice to wait for a day or two was again rejected, so I looked again in the cupboard, giving him something of a different colour. Once more, he did not get better. I thought it was too early to investigate his symptoms and looked again in the cornucopia in the wall. There were no more proprietary cough mixtures but there were several large bottles of brown glass, containing a variety of outdated medicines. Wedged among them was an out-of-date national formulary. I saw that one of the stock bottles contained 'Mist. Morph. Et Ipecac', which I remembered was supposed to be a cough medicine. I told the man I would see what I could do, and would hand in the medicine. Using ancient glass vessels, I mixed the above with something else I found in the formulary. I poured some of this into a smaller bottle, which I then corked and labelled. On the principle that if I survived it he would, I then took a dose of this concoction. It tasted horrible but produced no ill effects so the bottle was delivered as promised. I heard no more of him until he came back to have a loose tooth removed. This proved easier to deal with than his common cold.

A fortnight later I took a phone call from a woman in Uyeasound, at the south end of the island. 'I don't want you to come down,' she said, 'but could you give Postie a bottle of that medicine you made for Mr. X a wee while ago. He says it's really good.' It has been said that the only thing that separates man from other animals is man's desire to take medicine. It seemed that must be true, even for tough Shetlanders, and even if the medicine was a product of near antiquity.

Uyeasound was memorable for bad teeth and bad driving. I removed teeth which, happily, were loose, from several old Shetlanders, and had a call late one night about a car accident. It appeared that a van full of people had left the road and hit a wall. Nobody was seriously hurt but they had congregated after the accident in a nearby house. Eight people lived in the house and all were at home. The same number had emerged from the van. When I got there they were all in the living room, so the first thing to do was to ask all who had been in the accident to go into the other downstairs room. In spite of a suspicion that the travellers had greatly enjoyed the wedding reception they had attended, it did not take long to be sure that there were no significant injuries. But a more important matter then came to light. The owner of the van, which was a mess, asked if I was going to report this matter to the police, which meant the constable on the next island, Yell. I assured him that it had not even crossed my mind, and he seemed satisfied. The next morning I passed the scene of the crash on a separate call. In spite of the early hour, I saw that the wreckage had been removed and all the broken glass swept up.

Eventually the six weeks came to an end and sadly I had to leave Shetland. There was no longer any option but to decide on the next career move. It is the habit of the Navy to give everyone a copy of the report drawn up on him at the end of each commission. Mine was more than adequate, which meant that that a career in naval medicine would be possible. While this was an attractive proposition, the idea of giving up my freedom and having to go wherever I was posted for the rest of my working life, proved too much. I had also enjoyed the responsibility and varied nature of general practice. I decided, therefore, to settle for life outside the Navy, and to look back on my national service with the 3rd Frigate Squadron as something to be recalled with pleasure in the years to come. And so it has proved.